First World War
and Army of Occupation
War Diary
France, Belgium and Germany

2 DIVISION
Headquarters, Branches and Services
Commander Royal Artillery
1 October 1915 - 31 October 1915

WO95/1316/1

The Naval & Military Press Ltd
www.nmarchive.com
Published in association with The National Archives

Published by

The Naval & Military Press Ltd

Unit 10 Ridgewood Industrial Park,

Uckfield, East Sussex,

TN22 5QE England

Tel: +44 (0) 1825 749494

www.naval-military-press.com

www.nmarchive.com

This diary has been reprinted in facsimile from the original. Any imperfections are inevitably reproduced and the quality may fall short of modern type and cartographic standards.

© **Crown Copyright**
Images reproduced by permission of The National Archives, London, England, 2015.

Contents

Document type	Place/Title	Date From	Date To
Heading	B.E.F. France & Flanders 2 Division. H.Q. Commander Royal Art 1915 Oct To 1915 Dec.		
Heading	B.E.F. France & Flanders. 2 Division. H.Q. Commander Royal Artillery 1915 Oct To 1915 Dec.		
Heading	2nd Division Commdg Roy. Arty. Oct-Dec 1915		
Heading	2nd Div. R.A.H.O. War Diary October 1915		
War Diary	Lequesnoy	01/10/1915	16/10/1915
War Diary	Bethune (47)	17/10/1915	19/10/1915
War Diary	Bethune	20/10/1915	31/10/1915
Operation(al) Order(s)	2nd Division Operation Order No. 65	01/10/1915	01/10/1915
Operation(al) Order(s)	2nd Division Artillery Operation Order No. 5		
Miscellaneous	A Form. Messages And Signals.		
Miscellaneous	Daily Ammunition Return.		
Miscellaneous	2nd Division Artillery Orders by Brigadier-General G.H. Sanders D.S.O., Comdg. R.A. 2nd Division.	01/10/1915	01/10/1915
Miscellaneous	A Form. Messages And Signals.		
Miscellaneous	Daily Ammunition Return.		
Miscellaneous	2nd Division Artillery Order by Brigadier-General G.H. Sanders, D.S.O., Comdg R.A., 2nd Divn.	02/10/1915	02/10/1915
Miscellaneous	Brigade 28th Div	03/10/1915	03/10/1915
Miscellaneous	Bde Maj Pa 2nd Div	03/10/1915	03/10/1915
Miscellaneous	Daily Diary.	03/10/1915	03/10/1915
Miscellaneous	A Form. Messages And Signals.		
Miscellaneous	Daily Diary	03/10/1915	03/10/1915
Miscellaneous	First Corps Artillery. Registrations.	03/10/1915	03/10/1915
Miscellaneous	A Form. Messages And Signals.		
Miscellaneous	Daily Ammunition Return.		
Miscellaneous	2nd Division Artillery Orders by Brigadier-General G.H. Sanders, D.S.O., Comdg R.A., 2nd Divn.	03/10/1915	03/10/1915
Miscellaneous	BM Ra 2nd Divn.	04/10/1915	04/10/1915
Miscellaneous	Daily Diary	04/10/1915	04/10/1915
Miscellaneous	A Form Messages And Signals.		
Miscellaneous	Daily Diary. 44th Bde.	04/10/1915	04/10/1915
Miscellaneous		04/10/1915	04/10/1915
Miscellaneous	A Form. Messages And Signals.		
Miscellaneous	Daily Ammunition Return.		
Miscellaneous	A Form. Messages And Signals.		
Miscellaneous	Daily Diary	05/10/1915	05/10/1915
Miscellaneous	Bde May Ra 2nd Div	05/10/1915	05/10/1915
Miscellaneous	Daily Diary 44th Bde		
Miscellaneous			
Miscellaneous	B.M. 735	05/10/1915	05/10/1915
Miscellaneous	Bde May Ra 2nd Division	05/10/1915	05/10/1915
Miscellaneous	C Form (Original). Messages And Signals.		
Miscellaneous	A Form. Messages And Signals.		
Operation(al) Order(s)	7th Division Operation Order No. 47	05/10/1915	05/10/1915
Miscellaneous	Daily Ammunition Return.		
Miscellaneous	A Form. Messages And Signals		
Miscellaneous	Daily Diary	06/10/1915	06/10/1915
Miscellaneous	Bde May Ra 2nd Div	06/10/1915	06/10/1915

Miscellaneous	Daily Diary 44th Bde.	06/10/1915	06/10/1915
Miscellaneous		06/10/1915	06/10/1915
Miscellaneous	A Form Messages And Signals		
Miscellaneous	Daily Ammuntion Return.		
Miscellaneous	2nd Division Artillery Orders by Brigadier-General G.H. Sanders, D.S.O., Commanding R.A. 2nd Division.	03/10/1915	03/10/1915
Miscellaneous	A Form Messages And Signals.		
Miscellaneous	Daily Diary	07/10/1915	07/10/1915
Miscellaneous			
Miscellaneous	Bde Map Ra 25th Div	07/10/1915	07/10/1915
Miscellaneous	Daily Diary 44th Bde	06/10/1915	06/10/1915
Miscellaneous		17/10/1915	17/10/1915
Miscellaneous		07/10/1915	07/10/1915
Miscellaneous	A Form Messages And Signals		
Miscellaneous	Daily Ammunition Return.		
Miscellaneous	2nd Division Artillery Orders by Brigadier-General G.H. Sanders, D.S.O., Comdg. R.A. 2nd Division.	07/10/1915	07/10/1915
Miscellaneous	A Form. Messages And Signals.		
Miscellaneous		08/10/1915	08/10/1915
Miscellaneous	Daily Diary	08/10/1915	08/10/1915
Miscellaneous	Bde Map Ra 2nd Div		
Miscellaneous	Daily Diary 44th Bde		
Miscellaneous		08/10/1915	08/10/1915
Miscellaneous	Daily Ammunition Return.		
Miscellaneous	2nd Divisional Artillery Orders by Brigadier-General G.H. Sanders, D.S.O., Comdg. R.A. 2nd Division.	08/10/1915	08/10/1915
Miscellaneous	Programs Report	09/10/1915	09/10/1915
Miscellaneous	Daily Diary	09/10/1915	09/10/1915
Miscellaneous	Daily Diary 44th Bde	09/10/1915	09/10/1915
Miscellaneous		09/10/1915	09/10/1915
Miscellaneous	A Form. Messages And Signals.		
Miscellaneous	2nd Division Artillery Orders by Brigadier-General G.H. Sanders, D.S.O., Commanding R.A. 2nd Division.	09/10/1915	09/10/1915
Miscellaneous	Daily Ammunition Return.		
Miscellaneous	Brig Maj RA 2nd Div	10/10/1915	10/10/1915
Miscellaneous	A Form. Messages And Signals.		
Miscellaneous	Daily Diary.		
Miscellaneous	Daily Diary. 44th Bde	10/10/1915	10/10/1915
Miscellaneous		10/10/1915	10/10/1915
Operation(al) Order(s)	2nd Division Operation Order No. 57	10/10/1915	10/10/1915
Operation(al) Order(s)	7th Division Operation Order No. 48	10/10/1915	10/10/1915
Miscellaneous	Daily Ammunition Return.		
Miscellaneous			
Miscellaneous	A Form. Messages And Signals		
Miscellaneous	Progress Report. 31st Bde R.F.A.	10/10/1915	10/10/1915
Miscellaneous	Bde Map Ra 2nd Divn Progress Report	11/10/1915	11/10/1915
Miscellaneous	Brigade Major RA 2nd Divn	11/10/1915	11/10/1915
Miscellaneous	Daily Diary.	11/10/1915	11/10/1915
Miscellaneous	A Form Messages And Signals.		
Miscellaneous			
Miscellaneous	A Form. Messages And Signals.		
Miscellaneous	Daily Diary. 44th Bde.		
Miscellaneous		11/10/1915	11/10/1915
Miscellaneous	A Form. Messages And Signals.		

Miscellaneous	CRA II Division	10/10/1915	10/10/1915
Miscellaneous	A Form. Messages And Signals.		
Miscellaneous	Daily Ammunition Return.		
Miscellaneous	2nd Divisional Artillery Orders By Brig. Genl. G.H. Sanders, D.S.O. C.R.A. 2nd Divn.	11/10/1915	11/10/1915
Miscellaneous	Daily Diary	12/10/1915	12/10/1915
Miscellaneous	A Form. Messages And Signals.		
Miscellaneous	Daily Diary 44th Bde.	12/10/1915	12/10/1915
Miscellaneous			
Miscellaneous		12/10/1915	12/10/1915
Miscellaneous	2nd Divn. No. G.S. 657/5.	11/10/1915	11/10/1915
Miscellaneous			
Miscellaneous	2nd Division Artillery		
Miscellaneous	C.R.A. 2nd Div. Arty	12/10/1915	12/10/1915
Operation(al) Order(s)	2nd Division Operation Order No. 68.	12/10/1915	12/10/1915
Operation(al) Order(s)	7th Division Operation Order No. 49. by Major-General H.E. Watts, C.B., C.M.G., Commanding, 7th Division.	12/10/1915	12/10/1915
Miscellaneous	2nd Division R.A.	11/10/1915	11/10/1915
Miscellaneous	2nd Division R.A.	12/10/1915	12/10/1915
Operation(al) Order(s)	2nd Division Artillery Operation Order No. 6	12/10/1915	12/10/1915
Operation(al) Order(s)	Corrigenda to 2nd Division Artillery Operation Order No. 6	13/10/1915	13/10/1915
Map			
Miscellaneous	Daily Ammunition Return.		
Miscellaneous			
Miscellaneous	Daily Diary	13/10/1915	13/10/1915
Miscellaneous	A Form Messages And Signals.		
Miscellaneous	Daily Diary 44th Bde		
Miscellaneous	A Form. Messages And Signals.		
Miscellaneous		13/10/1915	13/10/1915
Miscellaneous	Daily Ammunition Return.		
Miscellaneous	2nd Division Artillery Orders by Brigadier General G.H. Randers, D.S.O., Cdg R.A., 2nd Divn.	13/10/1915	13/10/1915
Miscellaneous	Bde Map Ra 2nd Division	14/10/1915	14/10/1915
Miscellaneous	Bde Map Ra 2nd Divn	14/10/1915	14/10/1915
Miscellaneous	A Form Messages And Signals.		
Miscellaneous	Daily Diary	14/10/1915	14/10/1915
Miscellaneous	Daily Diary 44th Bde	13/10/1915	13/10/1915
Miscellaneous		14/10/1915	14/10/1915
Miscellaneous	Daily Ammunition Return		
Miscellaneous	2nd Division Artillery Orders by Brigadier-General G.H. Sanders, D.S.O., Comg R.A., 2nd Divn.	14/10/1915	14/10/1915
Miscellaneous			
Miscellaneous	Daily Diary 44th Bde RFA		
Miscellaneous	Daily Diary	15/10/1915	15/10/1915
Miscellaneous	A Form. Messages And Signals.		
Miscellaneous	Bde Maj Ra 2nd Divn	15/10/1915	15/10/1915
Miscellaneous	Brig Maj RA 2nd Divn	16/10/1915	16/10/1915
Miscellaneous		16/10/1915	16/10/1915
Miscellaneous		15/10/1915	15/10/1915
Operation(al) Order(s)	2nd Division Operation Order No. 69.	15/10/1915	15/10/1915
Miscellaneous	Daily Ammunition Return.		
Miscellaneous	A Form Messages And Signals.		
Miscellaneous	2nd Division Artillery Orders By Brigadier-General G.H. Sanders, D.S.O., Comdg R.A., 2nd Divn.	15/10/1915	15/10/1915
Map			

Operation(al) Order(s)	7th Division Operation Order No. 51. by Major-General H.E. Watts, C.B., C.M.G., Commanding 7th Division.	15/10/1915	15/10/1915
Miscellaneous			
Operation(al) Order(s)	7th Division Operation Order No. 52. by Major-General H.E. Watts, C.B. C.M.G., Commanding 7th Division.	16/10/1915	16/10/1915
Miscellaneous	Daily Ammunition Return.		
Miscellaneous	A Form. Messages And Signals.		
Miscellaneous	Daily Diary	16/10/1915	16/10/1915
Miscellaneous	Daily Diary 44th Bde R.F.A.	16/10/1915	16/10/1915
Miscellaneous	Bde Map Ra 2nd Divn.	16/10/1915	16/10/1915
Miscellaneous		16/10/1915	16/10/1915
Miscellaneous	A Form. Messages And Signals.		
Miscellaneous	Bde Map Ra 2nd Div Progress Report.		
Miscellaneous	Daily Diary.	17/10/1915	17/10/1915
Miscellaneous		17/10/1915	17/10/1915
Miscellaneous	A Form. Messages And Signals		
Miscellaneous	Positions to pic in ground from K5 to Canal		
Miscellaneous	Daily Ammunition Return.		
Miscellaneous	A Form. Messages And Signals.		
Miscellaneous	2nd Division Artillery Orders by Brigadier-General G.H. Sanders, D.S.O., Comdg R.A., 2nd Divn.	17/10/1915	17/10/1915
Miscellaneous	Bde Map Ra 2nd Div	18/10/1915	18/10/1915
Miscellaneous	Daily Diary 44th Bde. R.F.A.		
Miscellaneous	Daily Diary	17/10/1915	17/10/1915
Miscellaneous	Daily Diary 44th Bde R.F.A.	17/10/1915	17/10/1915
Miscellaneous		18/10/1915	18/10/1915
Miscellaneous	No 22 A.a. Section	18/10/1915	18/10/1915
Miscellaneous	Daily Ammunition Return.		
Miscellaneous	A Form. Messages And Signals.		
Miscellaneous	2nd Division Artillery Orders by Brigadier-General G.H. Sanders, D.S.O., Comdg R.A., 2nd Divn.	18/10/1915	18/10/1915
Miscellaneous	Bde Map Ra 2nd Div	18/10/1915	18/10/1915
Miscellaneous	Daily Diary 44th Bde R.F.A.	19/10/1915	19/10/1915
Miscellaneous	Bde Map. Ra 2nd Division	19/10/1915	19/10/1915
Miscellaneous	Daily Diary	19/10/1915	19/10/1915
Miscellaneous		19/10/1915	19/10/1915
Operation(al) Order(s)	2nd Division Operation Order No. 70	19/10/1915	19/10/1915
Operation(al) Order(s)	2nd Division Artillery Operation Order No. 7	19/10/1915	19/10/1915
Miscellaneous	Daily Ammunition Return.	19/10/1915	19/10/1915
Miscellaneous	2nd Division Artillery Orders by Brigadier-General G.H. Sanders, D.S.O., Comdg R.A., 2nd Divn.	19/10/1915	19/10/1915
Miscellaneous	Daily Diary	20/10/1915	20/10/1915
Miscellaneous	Daily Diary 44th Bde R.F.A.		
Miscellaneous		20/10/1915	20/10/1915
Miscellaneous	Daily Ammunition Return.	20/10/1915	20/10/1915
Miscellaneous	2nd Division Artillery Orders by Brigadier-General G.H. Sanders, D.S.O., Comdg R.A., 2nd Divn.	20/10/1915	20/10/1915
Miscellaneous	A Form. Messages And Signals.		
Miscellaneous	Daily Diary	21/10/1915	21/10/1915
Miscellaneous	Daily Diary 44th Bde R.F.A.	20/10/1915	20/10/1915
Miscellaneous		21/10/1915	21/10/1915
Miscellaneous	Daily Ammunition Return.	21/10/1915	21/10/1915
Miscellaneous	2nd Division Artillery Orders by Brigadier-General G.H. Sanders, D.S.O., Comdg R.A., Comdg R.A., 2nd Divn.	21/10/1915	21/10/1915
Miscellaneous	Daily Diary 56th Battery R.F.A.	22/10/1915	22/10/1915

Miscellaneous			
Miscellaneous	Daily Diary	22/10/1915	22/10/1915
Miscellaneous	C Form (Duplicate). Messages And Signals.		
Miscellaneous	A Form. Messages And Signals		
Miscellaneous	Daily Ammunition Return.		
Miscellaneous	A Form. Messages And Signals		
Miscellaneous	Daily Diary	23/10/1915	23/10/1915
Miscellaneous	Daily Diary 44th Bde RFA	22/10/1915	22/10/1915
Miscellaneous	R.A. 2nd Divn		
Miscellaneous		22/10/1915	22/10/1915
Miscellaneous	Daily Ammunition Return.		
Miscellaneous	2nd Division Artillery Orders by Brigadier-General G.H. Sanders, D.S.O. Comdg R.A. 2nd Divn.	23/10/1915	23/10/1915
Miscellaneous	Daily Diary	24/10/1915	24/10/1915
Miscellaneous	A Form. Messages And Signals.		
Miscellaneous	Daily Diary 44th Bde.	24/10/1915	24/10/1915
Miscellaneous	Daily Ammunition Return.	24/10/1915	24/10/1915
Miscellaneous	2nd Division Artillery Orders by Brigadier-General G.H. Sanders, D.S.O., Comdg R.A., 2nd Divn.	24/10/1915	24/10/1915
Miscellaneous	Daily Diary 56th Battery R.F.A.	25/10/1915	25/10/1915
Miscellaneous	Daily Diary	25/10/1915	25/10/1915
Miscellaneous	A Form. Messages And Signals.		
Miscellaneous	Daily Ammunition Return	25/10/1915	25/10/1915
Miscellaneous	2nd Division Artillery Orders by Brigadier-General G.H. Sanders, D.S.O., Comdg R.A. 2nd Divn.	25/10/1915	25/10/1915
Miscellaneous	2nd Division Operation Order No. 71	25/10/1915	25/10/1915
Miscellaneous	A Form. Messages And Signals.		
Miscellaneous	Daily Diary.	26/10/1915	26/10/1915
Miscellaneous	R.A.II Div.	25/10/1915	25/10/1915
Miscellaneous	Daily Diary 56th Battery	26/10/1915	26/10/1915
Miscellaneous	A Form. Messages And Signals		
Miscellaneous	Daily Ammunition Return.	26/10/1915	26/10/1915
Miscellaneous	2nd Division Artillery Orders by Brigadier-General G.H. Sanders, D.S.O., Comdg. R.A. 2nd Divn.	26/10/1915	26/10/1915
Miscellaneous	Daily Diary 56th Batt	27/10/1915	27/10/1915
Miscellaneous	A Form. Messages And Signals		
Miscellaneous	Daily Diary Z Group R.A.	27/10/1915	27/10/1915
Miscellaneous	Daily Ammunition Return.	27/10/1915	27/10/1915
Miscellaneous	2nd Division Artillery Orders by Brigadier-General G.H. Sanders, D.S.O., Comdg. R.A., 2nd Divn.	27/10/1915	27/10/1915
Miscellaneous	Daily Diary Z Group R.A.	28/10/1915	28/10/1915
Miscellaneous	FDA/40 Hqrs RA II Div.	28/10/1915	28/10/1915
Miscellaneous	A Form. Messages And Signals.		
Miscellaneous	2nd Division Artillery Orders by Brigadier-General G.H.Sanders., D.S.O., Comdg R.N. 2nd Divn.	28/10/1915	28/10/1915
Miscellaneous	Daily Diary 44th Bde RFA		
Miscellaneous	Daily Ammunition Return.	28/10/1915	28/10/1915
Miscellaneous	2nd Division Artillery Orders by Brigadier-General G.H. Sanders, D.S.O., Comdg. R.A., 2nd Divn.	28/10/1915	28/10/1915
Miscellaneous	R.A. 2nd Division.		
Miscellaneous	A Form. Messages And Signals		
Miscellaneous	Daily Diary Z Group Ra	29/10/1915	29/10/1915
Miscellaneous	Daily Ammunition Return.		
Miscellaneous	2nd Division Artillery Orders by Brigadier-General G.H. Sanders, D.S.O., Comdg R.A., 2nd Div.	29/10/1915	29/10/1915
Miscellaneous	Daily Diary. Z Group Ra.	30/10/1915	30/10/1915

Miscellaneous	A Form. Messages And Signals.		
Miscellaneous	Daily Ammunition Return.	30/10/1915	30/10/1915
Miscellaneous	2nd Division Artillery Orders by Brigadier-General G.H. Sanders, D.S.O., Comdg R.A., 2nd Divn.	30/10/1915	30/10/1915
Miscellaneous	A Form. Messages And Signals.		
Miscellaneous	Daily Diary Z Group RA	31/10/1915	31/10/1915
Miscellaneous	Daily Ammunition Return.	31/10/1915	31/10/1915

B.E.F. FRANCE & FLANDERS
2 DIVISION. H.Q.
COMMANDER ROYAL ART
1915 OCT TO 1915 DEC.

1316

B.E.F. FRANCE & FLANDERS.

2 DIVISION. H.Q.

COMMANDER ROYAL ARTILLERY

1915 OCT TO 1915 DEC.

2ND DIVISION

COMMDG ROY. ARTY.

OCT - DEC 1915

SUBJECT.

No.	Contents.	Date.
	2ND DIV. R.A. H.Q. WAR DIARY, OCTOBER, 1915	

WAR DIARY
or
INTELLIGENCE SUMMARY.
(Erase heading not required.)

Army Form C. 2118.

Hour, Date, Place	Summary of Events and Information	Remarks and references to Appendices
Friday 1.X.15 LE QUESNOY	Quiet day. No action of importance	
	2nd Division moved to NOYELLES and RA went under orders of	1306. 1307
	7th Division	1308
	36th Brigade rec orders to move and go under orders of 28th Division	1309
	Night firing orders	1310
	Ammunition Expenditure	1311
	Routine orders	
Saturday 2.X.15	Quiet day. No action of importance	
6.55f	Move of 36th Brigade complete	
	Night firing as last night.	1312
	Repair of enemys defences	1313
	Ammunition Expenditure	1317
	Routine orders	

WAR DIARY
or
INTELLIGENCE SUMMARY.

(Erase heading not required.)

Army Form C. 2118.

Hour, Date, Place	Summary of Events and Information	Remarks and references to Appendices
Sunday 3.X.15 LEQUESNOY	Quiet day on Division front but enemy attacked HOHENZOLLERN	1317a
	Plots drawn on registration	1315
	Orders issued for a reconnaissance of position in rear	1316
	Registration orders 44th Brigade	1317
	Report on repairs to refuges	1318
	Ammunition Expenditure	1319
	Routine orders	1320
Monday 4.X.15	Quiet day. Batteries occupied with registration and retaliation	1321
	Expenditure of Shrapnel too high. H.E. to be used	1322
	Report on enemy aeroplane work	1323
	Night firing orders - Ordinary defensive arrangements	
	Ammunition Expenditure	1324

WAR DIARY or INTELLIGENCE SUMMARY.

(Erase heading not required.)

Army Form C. 2118.

Hour, Date, Place	Summary of Events and Information	Remarks and references to Appendices
Tuesday 5.X.15 LE QUESNOY	Quiet day. No action of importance. Zones batteries registered. No work done by enemy. 2nd Div. O.O. 47 in reply RA not attached. Ammunition expenditure.	1325 ✓ 1326 ✓ 1327 ✓ 1328 ✓ 1329 ✓
Wednesday 6.X.15 ... 6pm	Quiet day. Arrangements for mutual support with registration. GOC attended conference at 2d. Army HQ Ammunition expenditure Routine orders issued	1330 ✓ 1331 ✓ 1332 ✓ 1333 ✓ 1334 ✓
Thursday 7.X.15	Quiet day. Arty. Lieut. E. Bocage 5 Nph. Addition to enemy's defences. Ammunition expenditure Routine orders	1335 ✓ 1336 ✓ 1337 ✓ 1338 ✓

WAR DIARY or INTELLIGENCE SUMMARY.

(Erase heading not required.)

Army Form C. 2118.

Instructions regarding War Diaries and Intelligence Summaries are contained in F.S. Regs., Part II. and the Staff Manual respectively. Title pages will be prepared in manuscript.

Hour, Date, Place	Summary of Events and Information	Remarks and references to Appendices
Friday 8.10.15 LE QUESNOY	Quiet day on our front. Bomb attack made on Guards and French. Attempted. Very windy. Wind E 5-10 m.p.h. Artillery activity to south	
	Wire.	1339
	Ammunition Expenditure	1340
	Routine orders	1341
Saturday 9.10.15	Misty day. Observation upon the enemy. Little wind.	1342
	All quiet.	
	Ammunition Expenditure	1343
	Routine orders	1344
Sunday 10.10.15	All quiet on our front.	
	2nd Division took over ground as far as G4A7 from the	
	Armentières Rd. Support invited by 31st Brigade and	1345
	our bakery 176th Brigade in action with 28th Divison relieving	1346
	Ammunition Expenditure	1347

WAR DIARY or INTELLIGENCE SUMMARY.

Army Form C. 2118.

(Erase heading not required.)

Hour, Date, Place	Summary of Events and Information	Remarks and references to Appendices
Monday 11.X.15 LE QUESNOY	All quiet on our front. Situation & miscellany.	1348
	Arrangements for supporting recent Bos.	1349
	Further request for support by Meerut Div.	1350
	Ammunition expenditure	1351
	Routine orders	1352
Tuesday 12.X.15	All quiet on our front. Continued miscellany.	1353
	Operation orders received for situation on 13th	1354
	do do issued	1355
	Ammunition expenditure	1356
Wednesday 13.X.15	Afternoon day spent in supporting attack by XI Corps on Fosse 8	1357
	Ammunition expenditure	1358
	Routine orders	1359
	Steady kept up all night on Hao alley, Auchy and Haisnes road.	

WAR DIARY
or
INTELLIGENCE SUMMARY.
(Erase heading not required.)

Army Form C. 2118.

Hour, Date, Place	Summary of Events and Information	Remarks and references to Appendices
Thursday 14.X.15	Day spent firing a barrage in Support of bomb fighting in HOHENZOLLERN. Very misty. Ammunition Expenditure Routine Orders Night firing as before.	1360 / 1361 / 1362
Friday 15.X.15	Barrage continued in Support of fighting in HOHENZOLLERN Very misty. All quiet on our front Orders for relief of 7th Bgde received Ammunition Expenditure Routine Orders	1363 / 1364 / 1365 / 1366
Saturday 16.X.15	Quiet day on our front. The Monstrelet in Support of fighting in Hohenzollern. Very misty. Orders for relief of 7th Division received Orders for relief and move of 2nd Div. HQ issued Ammunition Expenditure 7RA HQrs moved to 18 RUE SADI CARNOT BETHUNE and came under orders 2nd Division	1367 1368 1369 1370 1372

WAR DIARY or INTELLIGENCE SUMMARY

Army Form C. 2118.

Hour, Date, Place	Summary of Events and Information	Remarks and references to Appendices
Sunday 17.X.15 BETHUNE (47)	All quiet. Very misty. Busting position (Weekly return) Art'y fortune firing on GIVENCHY Ammunition expenditure. Night firing orders Routine orders issued	1373 1374 1375 1376 1377 1378
Monday 18.X.15	Quiet day, very misty. No action of importance. Situation unchanged. Ammunition received at Corps Artillery Conference Instructions issued for demand slips, and ammunition returns by G.O.C. to Brigades Night firing orders Routine orders	1379 1380 1381 1382

WAR DIARY
or
INTELLIGENCE SUMMARY.

(Erase heading not required.)

Army Form C. 2118.

Hour, Date, Place	Summary of Events and Information	Remarks and references to Appendices
Tuesday 19/10/15 BETHUNE (47)	Misty day. All quiet. No action of importance on our front. 2nd Division Operation Orders received. Operation orders No. 7 issued. Ammunition Expenditure. Routine orders.	1382ᵃ 1383 1384 1385 1386
Wednesday 20/10/15 BETHUNE	Misty day. All quiet. No action of importance on our front. Reliefs carried out. Ammunition Expenditure. Routine orders.	1387 & 1388 1389 1390
Thursday 21/10/15 BETHUNE	Misty day. No action of importance on our front. Reliefs carried out by 47 Bde. Ammunition Expenditure. Routine orders.	1391 1392 1393

WAR DIARY or INTELLIGENCE SUMMARY.

Army Form C. 2118.

Hour, Date, Place	Summary of Events and Information	Remarks and references to Appendices
22:10:15 Bethune	Misty day. Quiet day on our front. Registration carried out. Ammunition expenditure — Routine orders nil.	1394. 1395.
23:10:15.	Misty day. A certain amount of retaliation to M.G. squads & men observed firing carried out. Trench mortar located. Ammunition expenditure — Routine orders.	1396. 1397.
24:10:15.	Misty day. Retaliation for shelling by heavies & normal carried out. Ammunition expenditure — Routine orders.	1398. 1399. 1400. 1401.

Army Form C. 2118.

WAR DIARY
or
INTELLIGENCE SUMMARY.
(Erase heading not required.)

Instructions regarding War Diaries and Intelligence Summaries are contained in F. S. Regs., Part II. and the Staff Manual respectively. Title pages will be prepared in manuscript.

Hour, Date, Place	Summary of Events and Information	Remarks and references to Appendices
25:10:15 Bethune	Wet day light heat. No action of importance to report. Ammunition expenditure Routine orders 2nd Div. operation orders.	1402 1403 1404 1405
26:10:15	Fine day good light no action of importance on front. Ammunition expenditure Routine orders.	1406 1407 1408
27:10:15	Misty wet day bad light no action of importance on our front. Ammunition expenditure Routine orders.	1409 1410 1411

WAR DIARY
or
INTELLIGENCE SUMMARY.
(*Erase heading not required.*)

Army Form C. 2118.

Hour, Date, Place	Summary of Events and Information	Remarks and references to Appendices
28.10.15 BETHUNE	Wet day. With all day. No action of importance. Inspection by H.M. The King.	1412
	Ammunition return.	1413.
	Orders for registration in connection with 7th Div. operations at Givenchy issued.	Operations 2 1414
	Routine orders issued.	1415
29.X.15	S. Wind. Fine. No action of importance.	1416
	2nd Heavy Brigade relieved by ELLERSHAW's Brigade	1417
	Ammunition expenditure	
	Routine orders	
30.X.15	S. wind. Fair. No action of importance	1718
	Ammunition expenditure	1719
	Routine orders	1720
31.X.15	Very quiet day. Dull. Very bad light: much S.E. No action of importance.	1721
	Application for 600 hostile shells	1722
	Registration for Givenchy operation completed	
	Ammunition expenditure	1723

Copy No. 4

2ND DIVISION OPERATION ORDER NO. 65.
****

Reference BETHUNE Combined Sheet.1/40,000.
& Trench Map 1/10,000, Sheets
36.c.NW.1 and 3.   1st October, 1915.

1. 5th and 6th Infantry Brigades will today take over portion of the line G.18.b.4.4 and G.5.c.8.5 from 21st Infantry Brigade of 7th Division and 83rd Brigade of 28th Division as follows :-

<u>5th Infantry Brigade:</u> G.18.b.4.4 to strong point G.12.a.5.4 (exclusive).
<u>6th Infantry Brigade:</u> Strong point G.12.a.5.4 inclusive to G.5.c.8.5.

Arrangements to be made direct between Brigade Commanders concerned.
Completion of relief to be reported by 5th and 6th Infantry Brigades.

2. Artillery support for this line is being furnished by 7th Divisional Artillery.

3. 5th Field Company, R.E. is at disposal of 5th Inf.Brigade and 11th Field Company, R.E. at disposal of 6th Infantry Brigade.

4. No.15 Trench Mortar Battery will be attached to 5th Infantry Brigade and 1 section No.6 Trench Mortar Battery to 6th Infantry Brigade.

5. 2nd Division will take over the evacuation of this line under arrangements to be made direct between A.D's.M.S. of Divisions concerned.

6. 19th Infantry Brigade will be relieved tonight by 20th and 22nd Brigades of 7th Division under arrangements to be made direct between Brigade Commanders concerned. On relief 19th Inf.Brigade will be in Divisional Reserve and will send one battalion to LANCASHIRE TRENCH DUG-OUTS N. of VERMELLES, one battalion NOYELLES Line Dug-outs about G.1.b. and d, one battalion ANNEQUIN,F.29.d., 2 battalions SAILLY LABOURSE.
No.1 Section, 6th Trench Mortar Battery will remain attached to 19th Infantry Brigade.

7. Commands of the various lines will be taken over and handed over as the various reliefs are completed. On completion of the relief of the 19th Inf.Brigade, 58th Brigade of 19th Division will come under orders of G.O.C., 7th Division.

8. Advanced 2nd Divisional H.Q. will open at NOYELLES at 5 p.m. this evening and will also remain open at LE QUESNOY CHATEAU until relief of 19th Infantry Brigade is completed.

Louis Vaughan

Lieut-Colonel,
G.G.S.O., 2nd Division

P.T.O.

Issued at 10-45 a.m. to :-

    Copy No.1.... 5th Infantry Brigade.
      ,,   2.... 6th Infantry Brigade.
      ,,   3.... 19th Infantry Brigade.
      ,,   4.... R.A., 2nd Division.
      ,,   5.... R.E., 2nd Division.
      ,,   6.... Divisional Signal Co.
      ,,   7.... No.1 Bty. M.M.G.S.
      ,,   8.... Divisional Mounted Troops.
      ,,   9.... A.D.M.S.
      ,, 10.... "Q".
      ,, 11.... A.P.M.
      ,, 12.... Camp Commandant.
      ,, 13.... Adv. 1st Corps.   )
      ,, 14.... Adv. 19th Division.)
      ,, 15.... Adv. 28th Division.) For information.
      ,, 16.... Adv. 7th Division.)
      ,, 17.... Adv. 12th Division.)

S E C R E T.

2nd Division Artillery Operation Order No. 5.

7th Division assumed command today 1st October, 1915 at 5 p.m.

17th Battery and 47th Battery are rejoining the Divisional Artillery and will go into action in support of the Division.

On completion of the movement the artillery will be organized as follows:-

    Supporting 22nd Infantry Brigade. -
        31st Brigade - 69th Battery.
                   100th   "
                   103rd   "

    Supporting 20th Infantry Brigade. -
        41st Brigade. - 118th Battery.
                   9th   "
                   17th   "

    Supporting 58th Infantry Brigade. -
        34th Brigade - 50th Battery.
                   70th   "

    Covering whole front -
        44th Brigade - 47th Battery.
                   56th   "

The necessary changes will be adjusted by noon 3rd Octbr.

                                             Major, R.A.,

                             Brigade Major, R.A. 2nd Div.

Issued at........to:-

    31st Brigade.
    41st   "
    34th   "
    44th   "
    D.A. Column.
    7th Division.   )
    28th Divn. R.A.,) For information.
    Meerut Divn. R.A.)

"A" Form.   Army Form C. 2121.

MESSAGES AND SIGNALS.

Prefix ___ Code ___ m.	Words	Charge	This message is on a/c of:	Recd. at ___ m.
Office of Origin and Service Instructions.	Sent			Date ___
___	At ___ m.		___ Service.	From ___
___	To ___			
___	By ___		(Signature of "Franking Officer")	By ___

TO { R. A 2nd Div

| * Sender's Number | Day of Month | In reply to Number | |
| AFC 140 | 1-10-15 | | AAA |

Ref: First Corps Arty: operation order
No   para: 4 dated 30 Sept: 1915. aaa
1. Bde 18 pars of 2nd D.A. will relieve 50th Bde
R.F.A. by 10pm 2nd October and will
come under orders of CRA 28th Div aaa
Details of relief to be arranged between
C.R.As Second and Twenty eighth Divisions
aaa 50th Bde: R.F.A will be prepared to
march to rejoin 9th Div early on 3rd inst:
aaa. Acknowledge aaa
Addressed R.A: 2nd and 28th Divisions
Repeated 9th and 1st Corps

By Telephone

From	R.A 1st Corps.
Place	
Time	1-10 pm

The above may be forwarded as now corrected.   (Z)

Censor.   Signature of Addressor or person authorised to telegraph in his name
* This line should be erased if not required.

"A" Form. Army Form C.2121.

MESSAGES AND SIGNALS.

Prefix____ Code____ m.	Words	Charge	This message is on a/c of:	No. Message____
Office of Origin and Service Instructions.	Sent			Recd. at____ m.
_____	At____ m.		_____Service.	Date_____
_____	To____			From_____
_____	By____		(Signature of "Franking Officer")	By_____

TO { ~~H~~ 36 R.A. R.A Meerut Div:

Sender's Number	Day of Month	In reply to Number		AAA
BM 705	18th	(amdt orders)		
	Ree:	will	retire	5pm
a	but	10 p.m	2nd Oct	
ayd	will	come	under	orders
of	"A" 2nd Div.			
		36		
addressed	~~H~~	R.A:		
Repeated	Meerut Div:			
				(705)

From Second Div Arty
Place
Time 5.15 pm

The above may be forwarded as now corrected. (Z)
Censor. Signature of Addressor or person authorised to telegraph in his name

BM RA 2nd

"A" Form.   Army Form C. 2121.

MESSAGES AND SIGNALS.

Prefix____ Code____ m.	Words	Charge	This message is on a/c of:	Recd. at____ m.
Office of Origin and Service Instructions.	Sent			Date____
	At____ m.		____Service.	From____
	To____			
	By____		(Signature of "Franking Officer")	By____

| TO { | 3/ 3/4 | | | |

| * Sender's Number | Day of Month | In reply to Number | AAA |
| BM 711 | | | |

night	firing	as	last	night
aga		also	fire	at
the	rate	of	12 rounds
er	hour	will	be	kept
up	on	any	points	in
Divisional	front	where	enemy
is	known	to	be	working

(711)

| From Place | Second Div | Arty | |
| Time | | | |

The above may be forwarded as now corrected.   (Z)

Censor.   Signature of Addressor or person authorised to telegraph in his name

Major
BMRA 2Dn

* This line should be erased if not required

DAILY AMMUNITION RETURN.

19 Oct 15

Piece	Projectile	Code	B A T T E R I E S										Total	Per piece
			50	70	15	48	71	9	16	17	47	55		
2.75	Guns Shrapnel	P												
	H.E.	PX												
18-pr	Guns Shrapnel	A		17	18	21	19	16	16	39	9		342	
	H.E.	AX		27	4	–	4	3	20	–	–	38 9–	11 5
4.5" How.	Howitzers Shrapnel	B												
	H.E.	BX												
6" How	Howitzers Shrapnel	H												
	H.E.	F												
	A.P.													

B10

2nd Division Artillery Orders

by

Brigadier-General G.H. SANDERS, D.S.O., Comdg. R.A. 2nd Division.

1st October, 1915.

1021. REFILLING.

Supply wagons will refill from tomorrow inclusive on the BETHUNE FOUQUIERES ROAD, South of the level crossing, E.16a10.7. at the usual time.

1022. LEAVE.

Reference 2nd Division D.A. Order No 997 dated 18th Sept. 1915.

Until further orders the following will be the allotment of leaves :-

Sunday.	D.A. Column.	11.
Monday.	7th Mtn. Bty.	3.
	34th Brigade.	1.
	44th Brigade.	1.
	9th Siege.	3.
Tuesday.	36th Brigade.	5.
	41st Brigade.	5.
	D.A.Column.	1.
Wednesday.	34th Brigade.	11.
Thursday.	36th Brigade.	11.
Friday.	41st Brigade.	11.
Saturday.	44th Brigade.	11.

L.G. BUXTON, Capt.

Staff Capt. R.A., 2nd Division.

NOTICE.

FOUND.

Brown mare - about 15.3 hands - marked on off fore "B.6." - very poor condition - old collar, breast and trace galls.

Apply O.C., 44th Bde. Amm. Column.

"A" Form.
MESSAGES AND SIGNALS.

Prefix___ Code___ m.	Words	Charge	This message is on a/c of:	Recd. at___ m.
Office of Origin and Service Instructions.	Sent			Date___
	At___ m.		___Service.	From___
	To			
	By		(Signature of "Franking Officer")	By___

TO: ~~Inverness 31~~ ~~Zulu Camp~~ 31 4/4 Bde R.A.
~~By Chap 34~~ ~~Zulu Camp~~

Sender's Number	Day of Month	In reply to Number	AAA
BM 714	2nd		

First reply annex aaa hereinafter Report will be furnished each evening to R A 1st Corps by each Bde Arty on the Meaning subjects within its own zone aaa Additions or repairs to enemy defences including machine gun emplacements loopholes defended houses etc aaa New wire erected or old wire mended aaa Report to reach RA 1st Corps by 9 p.m aaa ends aaa This information should reach this office by eight p m daily aaa if the diary is not despatched in time to arrive here by 8 pm the information must be wired aaa acknowledge

From	Second Div Arty
Place	
Time	9-6 am

The above may be forwarded as now corrected. (Z)

Censor. Signature of Addressor or person authorised to telegraph in his name

Major
BM R A 2 Dn

"A" Form.   Army Form C.2121.

MESSAGES AND SIGNALS.

Prefix ___ Code ___ m.	Words	Charge	This message is on a/c of:	Recd. at ___ m.
Office of Origin and Service Instructions.	Sent			Date ___
	At ___ m.		___ Service.	From ___
	To			
	By		(Signature of "Franking Officer")	By ___

TO { R.A. 1st Corps

| Sender's Number | Day of Month | In reply to Number | |
| BM 716 A | 2 | | AAA |

Plans to enemy's defences aaa all gaps between TORTOISE and H Brickstack have been repaired aaa new wire observed S of point A21d77 aaa embankment about new wire aaa new wire is being erected behind old just north of LA BASSEE road aaa new MG emplacements at A16c28 and A16c46 aaa loopholes repaired along top of embankment and main trench from A16c46 to A15b35 aaa new sandbags between brickstacks and main road aaa new wire mixed with old from brickstack A to 50 yards N of road aaa thence repairs to old wire to 100 yards

From	South of road aaa
Place	RA 2 Div
Time	8.10 pm

The above may be forwarded as now corrected.   (Z)

Censor.   Signature of Addressor or person authorised to telegraph in his name

* This line should be erased if not required.

B13

DAILY AMMUNITION RETURN.

Piece	Projectile	Code	50	70	15	48	71	9	16	17	47	53				Total	Per piece
2.75	Guns																
	Shrapnel	P															
	H.E.	PX															
18-pr	Guns																
	Shrapnel	A	85	12	-	-	-	29	93	-	-	Total 103				615	
	H.E.	AX	70	-	-	-	-	14	6	-	-	Nil 28				238	
4.5" How.	Howitzers																
	Shrapnel	B															
	H.E.	BX															
6" How	Howitzers																
	Shrapnel	H															
	H.E.	F															
	A.P.																

2nd Division Artillery Orders

by

Brigadier-General G.H.SANDERS, D.S.O., Comdg R.A., 2nd Divn.

2nd October, 1915.

1023. COURTMARTIAL.

A F.G.C.M., will assemble at R.A., 2nd Divn, Hd.Qrs. F.8.b.9.3., at 10 a.m. on Monday, 4th October, 1915, for the purpose of trying No.10075 Dr. A.Williams, and No.49102 Gr. F.Rumsey, 47th Battery, R.F.A., and such other accused persons as may be brought before it:-

President.
Major R.ff.Powell.   71st Battery, R.F.A.

Members.
Captain R.Fernie.   2 Section, D.A.C.
Captain A.J.Clark.   1st Army. Hd.Qrs.
Lieut. G.Messervy.   16th Battery, R.F.A.

Accused will be warned and all witnesses to attend.

The 44th Brigade will furnish the Court Orderly and necessary stationery.

Proceedings will be sent to S.C.R.A., 2nd Division.

L.G.BUXTON, Capt, R.A.
Staff Captain, R.A., 2nd Divn.

Brig major RA 28th Divn

There was a disturbed night in the direction of LITTLE WILLIE but all was pretty quiet along 31st Bde front.

Parties of Queens Regt who were pulling up wire were annoyed by rifle fire so 100th Bty fired at German front trenches at 12.30 am and 1.20 am.

One of our Batteries was firing short into P3 trench (A 25 C 15) at 7.30 am & 8 am This was at once reported to 28th Divn R.A.

The 69th Battery fired at the point where LITTLE WILLIE joins German front trench at 7. am at request of R.W. Fusiliers

It would be of great assistance if we could be informed which 18 pr. Batteries are firing over LITTLE WILLIE trenches as this Brigade is unable to fire over them and have been asked on 2 or 3 occasions to stop by the Infantry.

9.0 am.
3/10/15

K J Ireland
Capt RFA
for O.C. 31st Bde RFA

B. Maj R.A. 2nd Divn   9.445

1. In continuation of my report of this morning the Queens Regt reported shells bursting short in their trenches at 11 am and 11.10 am. The 31st Bde Batteries were not firing at that time. They may have been German shell? At 2.10 pm Warwick Regt were worried by trench mortar. H.E. was fired in the direction reported but was ineffective as ~~the~~ position a mistake was made on the telephone. The mortar ~~stopped firing~~ fired very few rounds.

2. 69th Battery report that at 7.10 am the R.W. Fusiliers called them up at the instance of 1/Welsh and asked for fire at the same spot as last night i.e. at junction of LITTLE WILLIE and front trench. The Battery fired. Fire was asked for to stop bomb throwers. After ¼ hour. Infantry asked fire to cease and all was reported quiet except that a Battery continued to fire on our own trenches.

An aeroplane fight was seen between 2 British and one German aeroplane. The latter escaped.
It is hoped that the masses of men and horses N & W of VERMELLES escaped notice.
At about 5 pm much bombing was heard in the direction of HOHENZOLLERN and there

2

was heavy artillery fire both British & German.

J H Bud[?] Lt Col RA
Cmdg 3rd Bde RA[?]

3/10/15

No alterations in Enemy's wire noticed.

JHB

DAILY DIARY.

Z2 group.   3-10-15

9ᵗʰ Batt. 3-4 pm fired on working party in AUCHY and on road VERT FEUILLAGE to COR ONS. Some Germans and a transport wagon seen moving N A18d 9.0 Some Germans seen in Coron de PEKIN at 3.30 pm.

17ᵗʰ Batt registd. Fired at W. exit of Fosse 8 at Germans seen in open. Fired on German 2ⁿᵈ line at 4.52 pm by request, and near crater A21d 5.0 in response to german bombing.

118ᵗʰ Batt registered.

No new wire seen. No new works seen.
118ᵗʰ Batt took over from 103ʳᵈ Batt

Rodd th
Adj. Z2 group

⑲
7.25 PM

"A" Form.
Army Form C. 2121.

MESSAGES AND SIGNALS.

TO: Ra 2nd DIV.

Day of Month: 3

AAA

Daily Report 'A' 34th Bde
Enemy exploded a mine and broke in part of our parapet in A2. 50th B.Bty retaliated. 50th Bty retaliated to shelling of the BULGE during the day. 70th registered from new position. All damage done by bombardment has been repaired opposite A2 and EMBANKMENT REDOUBT and works to the South are as strong as they were before bombardment. All wire has been repaired but there may be a few very small gaps left. A length of pipe was seen this evening in front of enemy's parapet at A16C4.5½. This was fired at but light too bad to see the result.

Chefand
Capt.

DAILY DIARY
44th Bde.
6 p.m. 2nd – 6 p.m. 3rd Oct

Operations.

Nil.

Information

New work:— Pipe about 8" in diameter at A 16 c 4.5 running along trench for 30 yards visible at intervals. Sniper loophole on mound of earth at A 16 c 5.6. Parapet considerably strengthened around this point. Wire strengthened along the whole front. New machine gun emplacements just South of BRICKSTACK A. Several new loopholes and parapet strengthened between BRICKSTACKS & main road.

3.10.15

E.H. Harpur Lt. A. RFA
comg 44th Bde

6.55 PM

S E C R E T. 　　　　　　　　　　　　　No.1/R.A.S./1-92

FIRST CORPS ARTILLERY.
REGISTRATIONS.

The following registrations will be carried out to-morrow (if not already done) with Aeroplane where necessary:-

(A) 6" Howitzers.

    A sketch has been sent to Siege Group.

(B) 4.5" Howitzers.

    (i) 7th Divisional Artillery.

        SLAG ALLEY up to its junction with FOSSE ALLEY - 2 batteries.

    (ii) 28th Divisional Artillery.

        LITTLE WILLIE - 2 batteries.
        Communication Trench A.28.d.4½.2. - 8½.6. - 1 battery.

    (iii) 2nd Divisional Artillery.

        Communication Trench A.28.d.1½.5. - 4½.7½. - 1 battery.
        Communication Trench A.28.d.4½.7½. - 8½.6. - 1 battery.

As soon as these instructions are received communication will be opened at once with No. 3 Squadron R.F.C. with a view to arranging the necessary programmes.

3/10/1915.

                                Major, R.A.,
                        Staff Officer, R.A. 1st Corps.

Copies to:

2nd Divisional Artillery.
7th Divisional Artillery.
28th Divisional Artillery.
Siege Group.
No. 3 Squadron, R.F.C.
1st Corps.

"A" Form. **MESSAGES AND SIGNALS.** Army Form C. 2121.

Prefix____ Code____ m.
Office of Origin and Service Instructions.

~~Secret~~

| TO | 3" | Bde |
| | 4" | |

Sender's Number: 15m 725
Day of Month: 3
In reply to Number:
AAA

Please reconnoitre a position about 1000 yards in rear of your present positions for our battery

(725)

From: Ra 7 Div
Place:
Time: 6.40 pm

The above may be forwarded as now corrected.   (Z)   P. Munsberg Major

"A" Form.
MESSAGES AND SIGNALS.
Army Form C. 2121.

| TO | Aeronautics 3 | First Corps |

| Sender's Number | Day of Month | In reply to Number | AAA |
| 15 n 726 | 3 | | |

Please arrange to observe tomorrow for 47th and 56th Howitzer batteries who will register communication trench A28d 1½ 5 to 4½ 7½ and A28d 4½ 7½ to 8½ 6 aaa Details can be arranged with 56 Battery A20a 52 aaa both batteries can be joined

"A" Form.				Army Form C. 2121.
MESSAGES AND SIGNALS.			No. Message_____	

Prefix____ Code____ m.	Words	Charge	This message is on a/c of:	Recd. at____ m.
Office of Origin and Service Instructions.	Sent			Date_____
_____	At____ m.		_____Service.	From_____
_____	To			
_____	By		(Signature of "Franking Officer")	By_____

TO: 114th Bde

Sender's Number	Day of Month	In reply to Number	
19M.727.	3		AAA

47th & 56th Batteries are to register tomorrow on Trench A 28 d 1½ 5 to 4½ 7½ and A 28 d 4½ 7½ to 8½ 6 aaa aeronautics will observe in afternoon aaa We have asked him to manage details with 56 and suggested they can use 16th Mast for both Btys aaa Please arrange to have

From		
Place		
Time		

The above may be forwarded as now corrected. (Z)

Censor. Signature of Addressor or person authorised to telegraph in his name

* This line should be erased if not required.

"A" Form.   Army Form C. 2121.

MESSAGES AND SIGNALS.

Prefix _____ Code _____ m.	Words	Charge		No. Message _____
Office of Origin and Service Instructions.			This message is on a/c of :	Recd. at _____ m.
	Sent			Date _____
	At _____ m.		_____ Service.	From _____
	To _____			
	By _____		(Signature of "Franking Officer")	By _____

TO {

*	Sender's Number	Day of Month	In reply to Number	AAA

516 Bty wireless Mast at A24.c.7.7. aaa. Afternoon will suit best.

From
Place
Time

The above may be forwarded as now corrected.   (Z)

Censor.   Signature of Addressor or person authorised to telegraph in his name

* This line should be erased if not required.

"A" Form.   **MESSAGES AND SIGNALS.**   Army Form C. 2121.

TO: R. A. 1st Corps.

Sender's Number: 728
Day of Month: 3
AAA

New work by enemy aaa.
Z 1 Section nothing reported
Z 2 Section nothing reported
A Section all damage by bombardment opposite A2 and on Embankment Redoubt repaired and works as strong as before. aaa. All wire repaired though there may be a few small gaps left. aaa. Pipe about 8 inches in diameter at A 16 c. 4-5. running along Trench for 30 yards visible at intervals aaa. Snipers loophole on mound of earth at A 16. c 5-6 aaa. New M.G. emplacements just south of Brickstack A. aaa. Parapet

From: Strengthened.
Place: Second D. Artillery
Time: 8.20 p.

Major

DAILY AMMUNITION RETURN.

3rd Oct.

Piece	Projectile	Code	50	70	15	48	71	9	16	17	47	53	69	100	143	108	Total	Per piece
2.75 Guns	Shrapnel	P																
	H.E.	PX																
18-pr Guns	Shrapnel	A	70	21	-	-	73	12	93	-	-	243				38		
	H.E.	AX	72	90	-	-	90	-				10						
4.5" How.	Shrapnel	B																
	H.E.	EX							2									
6" How Howitzers	Shrapnel	H															550	
	H.E.	F															262	2
	A.P.																	

1319

2nd Division Artillery Orders

by

Brigadier-General G.H.SANDERS, D.S.O., Comdg R.A., 2nd Divn.

3rd October, 1915.

1024. REFILLING.

From tomorrow inclusive supply wagons will refill at the Place De La Republique and the top half of the MARCHE AU CHEVAUX BETHUNE. Time unchanged.

1025. COURTMARTIAL.

The following men will be tried by the F.G.C.M. ordered to assemble in R.A. Order No.1023, dated 2-10-1915 :-

No.4858. Dr.H.Gibbs. - 2nd Div. Ammn. Column.

No.82768. Fitter H.E.Lee. - 48th Battery, R.F.A.

1026. FIELD CASHIER.

The Field Cashier will attend at 7th Divisional Hd.Qr. Chateau de QUESNOY square F.8.b., between the hours of 10 a.m. and 1 p.m. on Monday, the 4th inst.

1027. RETURNS.

Reference G.R.O.1175, dated 27th September, 1915. Army Form B.213 and B.213a will be completed up to midnight on Fridays/Saturdays and forwarded with Army Form B.231 through the usual channels so as to reach this office by 9 a.m. on Saturdays.

L.G.Buxton, Capt, R.A.,

Staff Captain, R.A., 2nd Divn.

— B M Ra 2nd Divn —   G.51.

1. From 9 am until 11.30 am a large number of 5.9" shrapnel were fired over our trenches and area North of VERMELLES. It seems extraordinary that the area West of the village is not shelled as there are masses of men & horses there and there is every appearance of a fair or festival being held there. Our heavy guns and field guns replied to the shelling.

2. Observing station of 69th Bty in A 27 d 8.2 received considerable attention from whiz bangs. Machine gun located by 69th observer firing at one of our aeroplanes and this was fired on by the Battery & it desisted.

3. Party of Enemy seen to enter house in A 29 a 3.9. HE was fired at it by 69th F.

4. 100th Battery carried out registration.

5. 103rd Bty report that Germans fired into our trenches at 1.5 pm. They retaliated with HE.

6. 103rd Bty registered LITTLE WILLIE trench and also retaliated on trenches when rifle fire opened on our aeroplanes.

7. Nothing fresh has been noted in the Enemy's defences in the zone allotted to the

4/10/15   J H Budgen ?
                 Comdt 3rd Bde R F A

DAILY DIARY

Z 2 group.   4-10-15

9th Batt. shelled houses in AUCHY; clearing a field of view and shelled a cooking place. 3 pm.
   Repaired observing station.

17th Batt registered PEKIN trench and exits from Fosse 8 3.45 pm.
   3.25 pm a large dog running under German wire in front of LES BRIQUES left of VESUVIUS. He disappeared into German trench.

118th Batt. registered. Fired on front trench in retaliation to CRUMPS opp. 9.7.
   10 rounds were fired at battery 1/2 6" how. German balloon seems to have ranged battery.

(12)

F. Rodd
Adj. Z group.

T. Hop

	"A" Form.				Army Form C. 2121.	
	MESSAGES AND SIGNALS.			No. of Message..............		
Prefix......Code.......... m.	Words	Charge	This message is on a/c of:		Recd. at .... m.	
Office of Origin and Service Instructions.					Date	
	Sent		...................Service.		From	
	At............. m.					
	To					
	By		(Signature of "Franking Officer.")		By	

TO { Ra 2nd DW

Sender's Number.	Day of Month.	In reply to Number	AAA
BG/168	4		

Daily Report 34th Bde.
There was a good deal of rifle fire during the night chiefly just North & just South of our Zone — 70th Bty fired and 50th Bty fired on enemy's trenches on these occasions. Times — 12.30 am & 4.45 am — 70th Bty fired at working party at A22b 2.8 50th Bty saw a German in grey house behind right hand end of train in TRIANGLE and got a direct hit. No alteration was observed in German defences since yesterday.

Oldach
Capt

From B
Place
Time 7-40p

The above may be forwarded as now corrected.   (Z)

DAILY DIARY.
44th Bde.
6 p.m – 6 p.m 3rd – 4th Oct.

Operations.

56th Battery.

11.30 a.m Registered approximately trench A28d 1½.5 – 8½.6.

3.55 p.m. Corrected above with aeroplane observation.

47th Battery.

Registered various points from new position also trench A28d 1½.5 – 8½.6 with aeroplane

Information.

New work – Parapet strengthened and new wire put up along whole front CANAL – LA BASSÉE road last night.

(14)

E.H. Harpur Lt Cd. R.F.A.
Comdg. 44th Bde.

4.10.15. 7·50 p

78

Loss of Aeroplane Station

Return of Aeroplanes now & engaged.

Battle Plane	Wind Scouts	Remarks
now engaged	now eng'd of 13 Leopards	Battle Plane not/lost on today's action pm
3	2	36. Anaconda. + 3 + 5:30.

19/5
4/5

To Note loss, ere coming to A.A.Hr.

No. 22 Anti-Aircraft Section.

Shooting Report to 4 P.M. 4-10-15.

Time.	Objective.	Rounds Fired	Remarks.
3.20 P.M.	German L.V.G.	85.	
5.10 "	—	60.	

19/
4-15.

T C Newton
Capt: R.A.
Comdg: 22 A.A. Section

"A" Form.

MESSAGES AND SIGNALS.

Army Form C. 2121.

TO: ~~34~~ ~~HE~~
   ~~31~~
   31   41 Bdes:

Sender's Number: BM. 732
Day of Month: 4.

AAA

Expenditure of shrapnel continues to be much higher than that of HE. Every effort must be made to employ HE in preference to Shrapnel as when a greater proportion of HE is available.

From: 2nd D.A.
Time: 3.55 p.m.

Major

"A" Form. Army Form C. 2121.

MESSAGES AND SIGNALS.

Prefix ___ Code ___ m. Office of Origin and Service Instructions.	Words	Charge	This message is on a/c of:	No. of Message ___
	Sent At ___ m. To ___ By ___		___ Service. (Signature of "Franking Officer")	Recd. at ___ m. Date 13/5 From ___ By ___

TO { RA 1st Corps

Sender's Number	Day of Month	In reply to Number	
BM 733	4.		AAA

Additions to enemy's defences aaa new wire and fresh work on parapets all along front between CANAL and LA BASSEE road aaa no other change reported aaa

From R a 2 D n
Place
Time 7·55 pm

The above may be forwarded as now corrected.   (Z)

Censor. Signature of Addresser or person authorised to telegraph in his name

* This line should be erased if not required.

DAILY AMMUNITION RETURN.

Piece	Projectile	Code	50	70	15	48	71	9	16	17	47	56	3rd	Total	Per piece
2.75	Guns														
	Shrapnel	P													
	H.E.	PX													
18-pr	Guns														
	Shrapnel	A	27	77	-	-	-	18	34	45	-	279	64	544	
	H.E.	AX	25	89	-	-	-	-	-	93	-	44		251	
4.5" How.	Howitzers														
	Shrapnel	B													
	H.E.	BX									1	34	57	91	
6" How	Howitzers														
	Shrapnel	H													
	H.E.	F													
	A.P.														

"A" Form.   Army Form C. 2121.
MESSAGES AND SIGNALS.

| TO | Ra 2nd DW |

| Sender's Number. | Day of Month. | In reply to Number | AAA |
| BG/169 | 5 | | |

Daily Report A 34 Brigade

Observation possible about 5.30 am. Light got bad about 9am and got worse as the day went on. Batteries retaliated to shelling of our trenches. Our front very quiet.
50th Bty report a good deal of work done on third line running South from N.E. Brickstack.

Childard
Capt.

DAILY DIARY.

Z 2 group   5-10-15.

9th Batt. fired on Fires in german trenches at 11.30 am.

118th Batt. fired at request of 9th DEVONS in retaliation for bombing. Continued registration.

17th Batt. Did not fire.

Nothing to report.

[signature]
Adjt. Z 2 group.

— Bde Maj RA 2nd Divn. — G 468.

All quiet last night in front of 21st Infty Bde. Very wet and misty day and observation very difficult.

100th Bty retaliated at 7am on German trenches A 28 a 0.1 for fishing gang.

During the day, at irregular intervals, salvoes were fired at different points in German trenches (front & support) and also houses. The following is a list:—

LES BRIQUES
MADAGASCAR
LONE FARM   } 69th Bty
MAD ALLEY
House A 29 a 3.9
Registration 3 CABARETS

These salvoes were pure agression and to annoy the Hun & damage his works. JHB

A 28 c 4.9
A 29 a 0.5 } 100th Bty.
A 28 a 0.1

Front and support trenches in A 27 b. } 103rd Bty

At 5.30 pm 12 5.9" crumps fell close to 100th Bty position appearing to come from HAISNES.

5/10/15.

J H Bond Lt Col RA
31st Bde RFA

DAILY DIARY
44th Bde

6 - 6 for 4th - 5th Oct.

Operations   Nil.

Information.
                 Nil.

New 47th Bde position is nearly finished will be completed by mid-day tomorrow

E.H.Harpur Lt.Col.
Comdg 44th Bde.

No 22 Anti Aircraft Section.

Shooting Report to 4pm. 5-10-15.

Time.	Objective.	Adopted Remarks.

11-35
3

5/15.

T. Newton
Capt: RHA
Commdg: 22 A.A. Section.

81

No 22 - Aircraft Detail

Class of Airplanes Due 7 August

		Remarks
	Photograph	
	negatived due	
	7 August	arrive am Pm
1	10 Airplanes	1

I Nash Capt Res
23rd N Recon

B.M.735

Extreme limit of fire of batteries Z2 group.

9th Batt. La Bassée road to CORONS ~~at~~ at Fosse 8 ✓

118th Batt. Right limit line from Batt. position produced through A28D 7.0 Left limit line produced through A16a 2.7.

17th Batt. Lines produced through A27 b 8.8 and A15 d 5.2

5-10-15.

Rodolph
Adj. Z2 group.

1326

SECRET.

— Bde Maj RA 24th Division — G.455

Ref your B.M. 735 of todays date. The limits of fire of Batteries from their present Emplacements are as follows:—

69th Battery. Position C.8a 1.3
Right Limits { A 29 d 2·2 for right section
{ C 5 b 8·3 " left section
Left Limits { A 21 d 3·1 " right section
{ A 27 b 8·8 " left section.

100th Battery Position C 2a 6·4
Limits Centre of A 29 to A 21 d 10·8

103rd Battery Position A 26 a 0·6
Right Limits. Centre of C 4.
Left Limit all guns LOFT COTTAGE A 22 d 2·3
one gun can shoot 2 degrees and 2 guns 6 degrees left of this limit.

H.H. Bondfield Cockn
Comdt 31st Bde RFA

5/10/15

"C" Form (Original).   Army Form C. 2123 A.

MESSAGES AND SIGNALS.

Prefix ... C ... Code ... Words ...

Charges to collect £ 2 s. d.

Service Instructions: 34th Bde

Received From ...
By ...

Sent, or sent out At ... m
To ...
By ...

Office Stamp. 6 OCT 1915

Handed in at the ... Office, at 11 ... m. Received here at 11.3 ... m.

TO Ra 2nd Div

*Sender's Number	Day of Month	In reply to Number.	AAA
	5th		

Extreme southern limit of

fire of 70th Battery

extends to CEMETERY ALLEY

on a29a

3.M
11-3b

FROM 34th Bde RFA

PLACE

TIME 11.25.

"A" Form.
Army Form C. 2121.

MESSAGES AND SIGNALS.

TO: First Corps

Sender's Number: BM 745
Day of Month: 5
AAA

New work done by enemy. aaa A good deal of work on 3rd line running South from N.E. BRICKSTACKS

(745)

From: R.A. 2nd Div.

Copy No. 8

7th Division Operation Order No. 47.

5th October, 1915.

1. The Guards Division of the 11th Corps will, on the night 5th/6th October, take over the front now held by the 28th Division.

   The dividing line between the 7th Division and the Guards Division will be RAILWAY ALLEY (inclusive to the Guards Division).

   The G.O.C. Guards Division will take over the new line at 10.a.m. on the 6th instant.

2. The 58th Infantry Brigade will, on October 7th be withdrawn from its present line, and revert to the Indian Corps, the 7th Division taking over the line now held by the 58th Infantry Brigade.

3. The 21st Infantry Brigade will, by mid-day on October 7th, extend its left to about A.21.d.2.3. The exact point of junction being settled between G.O's.C. 20th and 21st Infantry Brigades.

4. The 20th Infantry Brigade will, by mid-day on October 7th, extend its left to RIDLEY WALK. The exact point of junction being settled between G.O's.C. 20th and 58th Infantry Brigades.

5. The 22nd Infantry Brigade will, by 7.p.m. on October 7th, take over from the 58th Infantry Brigade, the front from RIDLEY WALK to the CANAL. This relief will not commence till 1.p.m.

6. The 58th Infantry Brigade will, on relief, march to an area which will be communicated to them by the 19th Division.

7. All details of the above relief will be arranged direct between the Brigadiers concerned.

8./

8.   Brigadiers will assume command of their new sections as soon as the relief is completed.

9.   The Artillery of the 2nd Division will continue to cover the front of the 7th Division.

10.   The billeting areas under the above re-arrangement have been communicated separately.

11.   The 2nd Division are placing two battalions, which are billeted in BEUVRY, at the disposal of the 7th Division as a divisional reserve.   O.C's of these battalions will report the position of their Headquarters to 7th Divisional Headquarters by 8.a.m. on the morning of October 7th.

12.   The completion of the above reliefs will be reported to Divisional Headquarters.

F. Gathorne Hardy

Lieut-Colonel,

General Staff, 7th Division.

Issued at 12 noon to :-

A.D.C. (for G.O.C.)   Copy No. 1.
G.S.O.1.   " 2.
G.S.O.2.(Office copy).   " 3.
A.A.& Q.M.G.   " 4.
Signals.   " 5.
Cyclists.   " 6.
Divnl. Sqdn. N.H.   " 7.
2nd Divnl. Artillery.   " 8.
C.R.E.   " 9.
20th Inf. Brigade.   " 10.
21st Inf. Brigade.   " 11.
22nd Inf. Brigade.   " 12.
A.D.M.S.   " 13.
7th Divnl. Train.   " 14.
1st. Corps.   " 15.
2nd. Division.   " 16.
Indian Corps.   " 17.
19th. Division.   " 18.
Guards Division.   " 19.
58th. Infantry Brigade.   " 20.

DAILY AMMUNITION RETURN.

Piece	Projectile	Code	\multicolumn{10}{c}{BATTERIES} 5th Cpt	Total	Per piece
			50/70	15/48	71	9	16	17	47	56/94	78		
2.75"	Guns Shrapnel	P											
	H.E.	PX											
18-pr	Guns Shrapnel	A	4.3	—		87	—	24	39			193	
	H.E.	AX	59	63		29	—	—	14	13	—	288	
4.5" How.	Howitzers Shrapnel	B											
	H.E.	BX				—	—	—	1	—	—	1	
6" How	Howitzers Shrapnel	H											
	H.E.	F											
	A.P.												

1329

"A" Form.   Army Form C. 2121.
MESSAGES AND SIGNALS.

TO: RA 2nd Div

Sender's Number: BG/170
Day of Month: 6
AAA

Daily Report "A" & 34th Brigade.

Btys fired several times during the night at request of infantry in reply to shelling & bombing. 7.10 pm last night there was heavy smoke and our infantry suspected a gas attack. 70th Bty fired and a large fire started. It is thought a shell set a dugout on fire. Both Btys fired at portions of parapet on our front. A lot of sandbags & timbers were sent flying. Nothing fresh to report on our front. Observation not possible till 10.30 am and light very bad all day. Wind N.W.

Geldard
Capt.

Place: 12

DAILY DIARY

Z 2 group.   6-10-15

9th Batt. destroyed 6 houses in Northern row of houses 29 C 2.2.
    Are beginning to prepare new position 2 platforms ready.

17th Batt. Registered COROWS DEPEKIN au MARON. Registered also HAISNES church in order to enflade AUCHY-HAISNES road. This is all that can be done without aeroplane.

118th Batt. registered COROWS and generally checked registration.

    Germans are beginning to light fires in trenches but put them out quite readily!
    Germans fired on La Bassée road with Phzz bang near 34th Bde Hqrs cutting 41st Bde Bell telephone line.

(11)   H. Rodolphs
                                Adj Z 2 group

6/10/15 • Brig Maj Rawrdson — • G473

All quiet during the night. The infantry are gradually repairing and strengthening the wire along our front (22nd Inf Bde) The wire is at present thin but is continuous. 103rd Bty fired a salvo of H.E at 7.15 pm along main street of HAISNES. The 100th By fired 2 salvoes at 9.40 pm and 10.40pm at MINE POINT & KEEP in A 27 b 9.2 & 9.5.
At 7.45 am 69th retaliated on Auchy for a few shells fired into VERMELLES.
At 10.30 am 103rd fired at German front trenches to retaliate for rifle grenades & again at 1.30pm.
11.30 am 69th fired at German working party 29 a 3.10.
Later aftn registration was carried out as under:—
69th Battery Road SW of AUCHY   A 23 C 11
              Power House Fosse No 8   A 29. C 8.3
              Houses   A 29 C 3.7
              "   A 21
100th Battery Horse   A 29 C 2.7
103rd   Power House Fosse No 8
              CORONS de PEKIN.
              HAISNES TRENCH.
Germans shelled heavily trenches opposite HOHENZOLLERN and Central Boyau. Our guns retaliated. One Round seemed to cause an explosion beyond FOSSE No 8.

DAILY DIARY
44th Bde.
6-6 p.m. 5th - 6th Oct.

Operations.

47th Battery.

12.15 p.m. Registered LES BRIQUES
A 22 d 1.2 & A 29 a 0.5.

56th Battery,

2.30 p.m. Continued registration of houses N. N.W. of the DUMP.

Information

Nil.

E.A. Harpur B-M. R.F.A.
Comdg. 44th Bde.

6.10.15.

84

To 2 Anti Aircraft sector.

Return of Aircraft was 9 engaged

	Enemy Planes disposed of		Remarks
	Totally destroyed and forced down	Probably destroyed and forced down	
	1	1 Lt	West from Westerly 17.30 p.m.
		1 Lt Anne 21/1 N	1 Lt 17.30

T.N.O.T. Raffy D.A.
Coming 21 th....

(15)
10.35 P.M.

10½
6.15

No 23 Anti Aircraft Action.
Shooting Report to 7 P.M. 6-10-16.

Time.	Objective.	Rounds.	Remarks.
10.0 P.m.	German L.V.G.	4	

T.C. Newton Capt: R.A.
Comdg. 23 A.A. Section

10/6.16.

92

"A" Form. Army Form C. 2121
MESSAGES AND SIGNALS.

SECRET

TO: Meerut RA

Sender's Number: Nm 797
Day of Month: 6

Artillery Support we can afford you
3rd K Bde (Atgd 4 3) to fire on
TOWPATH ALLEY
Thence to fire Atba 2 3
PEKIN ALLEY
Conveyed attack was

Artillery Support you can afford us
9th Bde to fire on
TORTOISE & TOWPATH ALLEY
ENEMY'S FRONT REDOUBT
Railway to THIEPVAL Spur Atbd 31

Edward 505 A

Above provisionally arranged by brigade
Acknowledge

From: Rd XBde
Place:
Time: 10 am

"A" Form.
MESSAGES AND SIGNALS
Army Form C. 2121.

TO	31 Bde	41 Bde	
	34 Bde		

Sender's Number: BM 752   **Day of Month:** 6   **AAA**

Registration of Fittoning should be completed by midday evening aaa AUCHY–HAISNES road A.29.q.4.8 to HAISNES crossroads two batteries 103 and 70 aaa 103rd section half 70th battery half aaa HAISNES alley two batteries 118 and 17 aaa in face of AUCHY A.29.a.9.9 to A.22.d.5.4 100th battery aaa CORONS DE MARONS and CORONS DE PEKIN as far as 3 CABARETS fire batteries of 17 118 103 bdy aaa Brigade commanders 31st & 41st Bdes to allot zones in consultation in preparation for bombardment should it be ordered aaa

From: R.A. 7 Div
Place:
Time: 6 pm

752

The above may be forwarded as now corrected. (Z)

"A" Form.
MESSAGES AND SIGNALS.
Army Form C. 2121.

| TO | Corps | Aeronautics | 3 | First |

Sender's Number.	Day of Month	In reply to Number	
BM 753	6		AAA

following Require registration and your assistance if available aaa

118	Battery	(A24c8·5)	HAISNES. ALLEY. W
17	Battery	(A24c8·10)	" " E
70	Battery	(A24c8·2)	road A29b4·8 to A30a3·8
103	Battery	(A26a0·7)	Road A30a0·7 to A30b3·6

above batteries can be joined up to 16" and so get messages from your wireless mast if notice be given aaa please say when you can give time for this aaa addressed aero 3 Repeated 31st 41st and 34th Boles

From: RA 2nd DIV
Place:
Time: 6·25 PM

(753)

DAILY AMMUNITION RETURN.

6" How

Piece	Projectile	Code	50	70	15	48	71	9	16	17	47	56	3A(US)	Total	Per piece
2.75	Guns														
	Shrapnel	P													
	H.E.	PX													
18-pr	Guns														
	Shrapnel	A	10	-				11	72	47		147	82	370	
	H.E.	AX	51	43				104	-	149		109	36	400	
4.5" How.	Howitzers														
	Shrapnel	B													
	H.E.	BX								12	35			47	
6" How	Howitzers														
	Shrapnel	H													
	H.E.	F													
	A.P.														

1333

2nd Division Artillery Orders

by

Brigadier-General G.H. SANDERS, D.S.O., Commanding R.A. 2nd Division.

6th October, 1915.

1028. R.A. ORDERS.

Were not issued on 4th and 5th October, 1915.

1029. INDENTS.

Divisional, Army Corps Troops and Army Troops Ordnance Officers will be the medium through whom all indents should be submitted by the troops.

Indents from units allotted, even temporarily, to formations will be submitted to the Ordnance Officers of those formations, unless otherwise decided by the Army Commander.

Indents for troops in G.H.Q. area will normally be submitted to D.A.D.O.S., G.H.Q. Troops.

Indents for all stores and clothing required in replacement must bear a certificate from the Commanding Officer that the articles to be replaced were expended or worn out on service.

G.R.O. No 625 is cancelled.

L.G. BUXTON, Capt. R.A.,
Staff Captain, R.A. 2nd Division.

"A" Form.   Army Form C. 2121.
MESSAGES AND SIGNALS.

| TO | Ra 2nd DIV |

| Sender's Number. | Day of Month. | In reply to Number | AAA |
| BG/172 | 7 | | |

Daily Report A 34th Brigade —

50th Bty fired a few rounds during night at request of infantry — 70th Bty fired at minenwerfer South of main road at 3.30pm and registered AUCHY - HAISNES road with an aeroplane.

A quiet day on our front About 8pm last night there was a good deal of firing in HOHENZOLLERN direction. As soon as fire stopped following lights were sent up — 1 green 2 reds 1 green in quick succession followed after 1 minute by 1 red.

Observation impossible 6pm — 8.45am

Reldaw
Capt.

Daily Diary.

22 group.   7-10-15

118th Batt fired several times during night on front trenches MINE Pt to pt 9.7 to stop bombing. Registered HAISNES alley with aeroplane.

17th Batt Fired on party of germans at a 29 C 2.9½ at 10.5 am. Registered comm. tr. around 3 CABARETS. at 12.30 pm fired on german front line at request of infants. Registered on HAISNES.

9th Batt. Registered CORONS DE PEKIN etc. Work done on rear position 4 platforms ready. 1 pit rebuilt in present position.

7-25%

GENERAL

No other movements of troops visible. At 1 p.m. an explosion took place behind MINE point a column of white smoke was observed.

Yesterday germans put a few 6" in our front trenches just S. of MINE Pt.

F. Rodd Lt.
Adj. Z ngroup.

Bde Maj R 28th Divn — 79

Nothing of importance during the night 6/7th
100th Bty fired a few rounds at request of
infantry at 7.50 pm. A few rounds were
also fired by this Battery at night to
annoy the Germans. 103rd Bty fired a
few rounds along HAISNES – AUCHY rd at
7 pm.
At 10.25 am 103rd Bty observer saw a fairly large
explosion in what appeared to be our front
trenches in A 20 C. There was a large cloud of
white smoke which lasted for ½ an hour
It seemed to cause no excitement.
At 11.45 several 9" shell were fired into
VERMELLES. The 69 Battery retaliated
as also for whizbangs on two occasions.
Registration was carried out as under
69th Bty. A 22 a Commn trench E of BRICKSTACKS
                    (support of 34th Bde)

            A 29 c 8.7   Houses
            A 28 b 4.1   House in MADAGASCAR
100th Bty. A 22 d 3.1   LEAF COTTAGE
            A 23 c 2.1   HOUSE S of AUCHY
            A 29 c 2.3   CORON at FOSSE No 8
            A 29 a 9.7   CEMETERY at AUCHY
            A 22 b 10.4   House and S of AUCHY
            A 29 c 8.3   Power House FOSSE No 8
            A 29 c 4.9   CORON de MARON.
103rd Bty registered point P with aeroplane and fired one
round at Q when telephone broke down and aeroplane went home
7/10/15   H.S.B. md L Col Cmy 28th Div

DAILY DIARY.
44th Bde
6-6 pm. 6th - 7th Oct.

Operations.

56th Battery.
8.12 am. Fired at Minenwerfer at A 21b 9.8 at request of infantry.

47th Battery.
5.15 pm Registered howzer at A 29 c 3.2.

Information.

Further additions to wire & parapets on EMBANKMENT REDOUBT and at A 16 c 2.8.

H Mand Capt Lt-Col R.F.A.
Comdg. 44th Bde.

No 12 of Aircraft Report

Return of Airplanes seen & engaged

Actual Planes Engaged	Much Practice was spotty	Hostile Planes dispersed when fired on	Remarks
1			
	11. Annexan -	2 6/30	

T.C. North
Capt. 11027
Comdg 22AA bde

18
9.45 pm

M 12/5
11 12.

No 22 Anti-Aircraft Section.

Shooting Report to 4 p.m. 4·10·15.

Time	Objective	Rds fired	Remarks

T C Newto
Capt. RMA
Comdg. 22 A.A. Section

4/15.

"A" Form. Army Form C. 2121.
MESSAGES AND SIGNALS.

TO	First Corps R.A.

Sender's Number.	Day of Month	In reply to Number	
BM 770	4		AAA

Addition to enemy's works aaa. Further additions to wire and parapet on EMBANKMENT REDOUBT and at A.16.C.2.8

770
7-56 pm

From: RA 2 Div.
Place:
Time: 7-55 pm.

Major
BMRA 2 Div

DAILY AMMUNITION RETURN.

7th Oct 1915

Piece	Projectile	Code	\multicolumn{11}{c}{BATTERIES}	Total	Per piece
			50	70	15	48	71	9	16	17	47	55	3/84		
2.75	Guns														
	Shrapnel	P													
	H.E.	PX												312	
18-pr	Guns														
	Shrapnel	A			6	4	—	—	9	110	50	—	104	29	
	H.E.	AX			12	15	—	—	88	2	16	—	105	80	409
4.5" How.	Howitzers														
	Shrapnel	B							1				6	12	
	H.E.	BX							1						18
6" How	Howitzers														
	Shrapnel	H													
	H.E.	F													
	A.P.														

1337

2nd Division Artillery Orders

by

Brigadier-General G.H.SANDERS, D.S.O., Comdg. R.A. 2nd Division.

7th October, 1915.

1030. ARMY FORM B. 213.

Reference G.R.O. No 1175 dated 27th September, 1915. A.F. B 213 should be forwarded by Os.C., Units to this office by 12 noon on Saturday of each week.

The perforated sheet attached cancels the usual return of <u>deficiencies</u> in personnel and horses rendered, but a return of <u>surpluses</u> will continue to be rendered to this office.

1031. FUZE NO 85 - STRIPS for INDICATOR.

Strips for fuze indicators for number 85 fuze are now available. Indents should be submitted to D.A.D.O.S. 2nd Division on the scale of one strip for each indicator.

L.G. BUXTON, Capt. R.A.,
Staff Capt. R.A. 2nd Division.

"A" Form.
MESSAGES AND SIGNALS.
Army Form C. 2121.

TO	RA 2nd Div.

Sender's Number.	Day of Month.	In reply to Number	AAA
BG/174	8		

Daily Report A 34th Brigade.

About 4.30 am Heavy bombardment of GIVENCHY started, and kept on till 5.15 am. 50th Bty fired a few rounds on PLAIN ALLEY. 70th Bty fired at working party A21 b 8.7 at 9.30 am. From 12 noon - 12.30 pm our front was bombarded with light field guns light & heavy howitzers till about 4.30 pm. 50th & 70th Bty replied at intervals chiefly on 2nd line & communication trenches. After 4.30 pm the bombardment was confined to direction of LOOS where the real attack seems to be. Our front is being shelled at intervals now but not heavily.

From: Observation impossible 5.30 pm - 7.30 am
Place: Rather misty day.
Time:

Goldney
Capt.

7.45

British. The retaliation appeared very lavish. VERMELLES was shelled and 69th Battery had an unpleasant time.
All Batteries retaliated at intervals at request of the Infantry
2 Red Flares were observed at 5.20pm in the direction of LITTLE WILLY. From 1st Army Intelligence Summary No 268 the nearest thing this could represent is "The enemy is attacking"

J.H.Bond J.Coe RFA
8/10/15 .   Cmdg 31st Bde RFA

A message was received from 21st Inf Bde at 1pm that Germans had been seen cutting their wire near Hill 70 and that Artillery were to be prepared

11

7.35pm

DAILY DIARY

Z2 group   8-10-15

9ᵗʰ Batt. Fired on CORONS DE PEKIN destroying some house. Also fired on suspected O.P. in AUCHY 3 p.m. Retaliated for German fire

17ᵗʰ Batt. retaliated for German fire on our trenches and registered LES BRIQUES

118ᵗʰ Batt. Fired on CORONS DE PEKIN and on MINE Pt to stop bombing.

Light much too bad to do much shooting all day. Germans shelled our trenches and communication trenches all over Z2 front commencing with light fire at 12.30 pm and increasing in intensity between 2 pm and 4 pm. Some rifle fire heard near Hohenzollern. Some Phizz-bangs near Fosse 9 otherwise not much shelling in rear part of Z 2.

R Roddah
Adj. Z2 group.

(12)

7·40 pm

G.48.

Brig Maj RE 2nd Divn — Progress Report.

At 6pm last night 100th Bty fired on a machine gun Emplacement on railway line in A28c0.1½ and again at 9.55pm. Machine guns from about this point I understand enfiladed the attack on Fosse No 8. The OC 100th Bty has heard from an Infantry officer who was present at this attack that machine guns from this point caused many casualties. There are also reports that the emplacements are concreted and if that is the case & they can be accurately located the 6" How wd be very useful.

The 103rd fired a few rounds between 6.15 & 7pm along HAISNES AUCHY Road.

The 100th Battery also fired half a dozen rounds during the night.

During the day registration was carried out on Buildings of FOSSE No 8 and was on the whole successful but bad light and the constant shelling of the whole front by our Arty made it difficult. A few rounds in good light to check the registration are reqd before a bombardment & this will be carried out tomorrow morning.

A continuous Artillery duel has been in progress since about 11.30am — the majority of the ammn expended appearing to be

DAILY DIARY
44th Bde.
6 - 6 pm. 7th - 8th Oct.

Operations.

47th Battery.

9.30 am. Registered with aeroplane communication trench A 28 d 8.6 & A 29 c 2.6.

2.30 pm. Registered 3 houses at A 29 C 4.8. and DIAMOND DOOR COTTAGE. A 22 d 8.8.

56th Battery.

6 pm. Fired at Minniewerfer at A 21 B 9.8 at request of infantry.

11.15 am. Shelled CULVERT in retaliation to shelling of HOLLOW by 150 mm How.

12.45 pm. Fired on communication trench & CULVERT in retaliation for shelling of HOLLOW.

2.40 pm.
& 2.55 - 4.20 pm. } — ditto — —

1.25 - 1.45 pm }
& 2.10 - 2.15 pm } Shelled barges in CANAL DOCK in retaliation to 150 mm on HOLLOW

Information:-
Our trenches in A 27 a & b and A 21 c & d were shelled all day with 77 mm & 105 mm shells.

H Hillard Cpt B.C., R.F.A.
Comdg. AA 4th Bde

90

Loss of 70- Sunday sketches &
others of dispatches sent & engaged.

		Head Posts of Trost of	Remarks
		dispatches and Posts of Sand Posts	3×3
1	16. Anzburn	1	
1		1	

T C Nutler

Capt. R.E.
O/c 20/A.R.E.

No. 22 A○A Aircraft Action.

Shooting Report to 7 P.M. 5·10·15.

Time	Objective	Rds fired	Remarks
2.30 P.m.	German L.V.G.	4.	

T C Newton
Capt. RMA
Comdg. 22 AA Section

6/15.

No 22 AA Section

DAILY AMMUNITION RETURN.

8th October 1915

Piece	Projectile	Code	50	70	15	48	71	9	13	17	47	53	3/64	1/88	Total	Per piece
2.75	Shrapnel	P														
	H.E.	PX														
18-pr	Guns															
	Shrapnel	A	4	40				16	364	179	—	—	145	22	770	
	H.E.	AX	181	86				123	9	19	—	—	385	128	931	
4.5" How.	Howitzers															
	Shrapnel	B														
	H.E.	BX								36	50				86	
6" How	Howitzers															
	Shrapnel	H														
	H.E.	F														
	A.P.															

2nd Divisional Artillery Orders

by

Brigadier-General G.H. SANDERS, D.S.O., Comdg. R.A. 2nd Division.

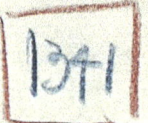

8th October, 1915.

1032. RIFLES.

Os.C., Brigades will report by 10th inst. whether the number of rifles now held, viz:- 10 per battery and Nil per brigade headquarters is sufficient during active operations. If it is considered that above is not sufficient, Os.C., Brigades will report the number of rifles which they consider is necessary.

1033. COURTMARTIAL.

A F.G.C.M. composed as under will assemble at Headquarters 2nd Divisional Artillery at 10 a.m. on Monday October 11th., 1915, for the trial of No 18986 Sergt. J. Ashe, 2nd D.A.C. and No 5027 Dr. Alfred Henker, 23 New Heavy Battery, R.G.A., and such other accused as may be brought before it :-

PRESIDENT.
Major C.D.G. LYON, 16th Battery, R.F.A.

MEMBERS.
Capt. B.L. MARRINER, 15th Battery, R.F.A.
A Subaltern to be detailed by O.C., 2nd Hy. Brigade.

The accused will be warned and all witnesses required to attend.
Proceedings to be sent to S.C.R.A., 2nd Division.
O.C., 2nd D.A.C. will find the Court Orderly and necessary stationery.

1034. ROAD CONTROL.

Men in charge of horses or of any vehicles, whether horsed or M.T., are on no account to halt outside estaminets and similar places, or to leave their animals or vehicles unattended on the roadside.

L.G. BUXTON, Capt. R.A.,
Staff Capt. R.A., 2nd Division.

Progress Report 9.10.15. C/857

At 7.0 p.m. last night the 103rd Battery fired on transport at HAISNES and at 8.45 p.m. on the German trenches in their zone to check enemy's rifle fire on our working parties.

The rest of the night was quiet, and the day has been too misty for observation. The 69th Battery attempted to carry out further registration of the CORONS DE MARONS from the front trenches without much success.

The 100th Battery fired about 50 rounds in the afternoon on the enemy's trenches and works.

LB
Lt Bond
Comdt 31st Bde RFA

9/10/15

9
7-55

DAILY DIARY

9-10-15   Z 2 group.

9th Batt Nothing to Report.

17th Batt. did not fire.

118th Batt. retaliated for Phizz bangs and registered. Fired on CORONS.

Too musty to see any thing impossible to state if any new work done. Equally impossible to state what damage has been done on the CORONS.
Some Phizz bangs were shot at our front trenches as above.

Rodd M.
Adj. 41st Bde.

DAILY DIARY.
44th Bde
6-6 pm. 8th - 9th Oct. 1915

Operations.

Nil.

Information

Nil. Too misty for observation. No hostile shelling reported.

9.10.15   HHMarlcot B.P.R. R.F.A.
                       Comdg. 44th Bde.

7.30 pm

No 22 Jy 6 - Away ticket.
Return of England Cash & cheques

	Phone Bill Codes un Spain	Monthly Return for	Annuals
		— ANNEQUIN. —	
	—		

T C Nesto
Locky Paul
money Bank A/C

11
9.30 pm

No 22 Anti Aircraft section.

Shooting Report to 9 PM 9/10/15.

Time	Objective	Ragfires	Remarks

T Nestor Capt: RHA
Comdg: 22 (A.A.) section

9/10/15.

"A" Form.   Army Form C. 2121.
MESSAGES AND SIGNALS.   No. of Message

TO: R.A. 2nd Division

Sender's Number: B.G./175

AAA

Progress Report 5.30 pm 8th & 5.30 pm 9th

50th Bty } Neither of the batteries have fired
70th Bty }

Very misty all day nothing of importance has transpired

Accurate observation impossible since 5.20 pm 8th

J. H. Lewis
2nd Lieut
34th Brigade
R.F.A.

10
7.50 p.

2nd Division Artillery Orders

by

Brigadier-General G.H.SANDERS, D.S.O., Commanding R.A. 2nd Division.

9th October, 1915.

1035. AMMUNITION RETURNS - RENDITION OF.

Os.C., units are reminded that all echelons should be as full as possible at noon on Sunday and that returns are due to reach this office at 3 p.m.

The daily return of ammunition on hand is no longer required except from B.A.Cs. and D.A.C.

L.G. BUXTON, Capt. R.A.,
Staff Capt. R.A., 2nd Division.

DAILY AMMUNITION RETURN.

9th Oct 1915

Piece	Projectile	Code	50	70	15	48	171	9	16	17	47	53	31st Bde Bty	Total	Per piece
2.75	Guns Shrapnel	P													
	H.E.	PX													
18-pr	Guns Shrapnel	A	8						2	8			94 31	133	
	H.E.	AX	8							1			170 112	291	
4.5" How.	Howitzers Shrapnel	B													
	H.E.	BX													
8" How	Howitzers Shrapnel	H													
	H.E.	F													
	A.P.														

1943

— Brig. Maj. RA 2nd Divn — Progress Report.

At 6.30pm ~~yesterday~~ 103rd Bty fired a few rounds along HAISNES AUCHY Road. At 7.30pm the Infantry reported to F.O.O. that they heard transport on this road. The Battery searched the road with H.E. and Shrapnel. Infantry reported transport much disturbed and galloping. At 11.30pm Infantry again reported transport on the road and a few more rounds of H.E. and Shrapnel were fired.

A few rounds of H.E. and shrapnel were fired into the front and communication trenches by the 100th Bty between 6pm and 10.30pm. Night on the whole very quiet.

Registration of Fosse No 8 and houses near it carried out during the day by 69th Bty. Wire cutting was not carried out as BC was held up in the communication trenches by the relief of Infantry. Observation of wire in his zone has to be carried out from near the support trenches.

100th Bty retaliated once or twice on the German trenches. Registration of Fosse 8 buildings was afterwards carried out. Wire cutting was also commenced but stopped owing to it being reported to the BC who was observing from the trenches that H.E. shell had fallen in our trenches and caused casualties to the Infantry

2.

A separate report is forwarded about these shell.
The 103rd Battery fired on the buildings of FOSSE 8 and registered the new night lines.

Heavy firing heard all the aftn from direction of LOOS.

5th Inf Bde took over trenches in front of the Bde during the aftn.

The 75th and 145th Btys of the 146th Bde are allotted to the Bde to assist in defence of the front of 5th Inf Bde.

Communication was arranged for with these Batteries and the F. Liaison offr of 146th in the Btn H.Q. of the Right Btn opposite LITTLE WILLIE was relieved by an officer of this Bde.

10/10/15

JH Smith Lt Col RA
Cmd 13th Bde RA

"A" Form.				Army Form C. 2121.
MESSAGES AND SIGNALS.				No. of Message

Prefix	Code	m.	Words	Charge	This message is on a/c of:	Recd. at	m.
Office of Origin and Service Instructions.			Sent			Date	
			At	m.	Service.	From	
			To				
			By		(Signature of "Franking Officer.")	By	

TO Ra 2nd SW

Sender's Number.	Day of Month.	In reply to Number	AAA
* BG/177	10		

Daily Report A 34 Brigade.

50th Bty fired at snipers post on the bankment.

70th Bty at 2.30pm retaliated to shelling of A1. 3.35pm registered buildings N.E. of force no. 8 – 4.15pm started firing on wire just North of main road.

Observation just possible at 6am but very misty till noon. After noon light very good. Our front very quiet. A German aeroplane passed over trenches about 5pm South to North, turned and came back but was driven East by our anti aircraft fire.

From
Place
Time 23/10

C Seldud
Capt.

The above may be forwarded as now corrected. (Z)

Censor. Signature of Addressor or person authorised to telegraph in his name.

* This line should be erased if not required.

DAILY DIARY.

Z. group.

10-10-16

9th Batt. Bombarded CORONS de PEKIN and registered points in DOUVRIN. Retaliated on AUCHY and fired on front trenches. Most of firing done in afternoon.

17th Batt. Fired on CORONS in morning light shewed considerable damage done. Fired on German wire and parapet till light failed (88 rds) Registered Centre of three P. Hs.

118th Batt. fire on houses S.W. of CORONS de PEKIN which former are now nearly demolished. Also in latter part of afternoon fired on German front trench demolishing a portion.

GENERAL.

Light poor in earlier part of morning became better during afternoon.

No new work has been reported.

"A german aeroplane flew over batteries this evening at about 5.15pm. None of our machines took any notice of it.

A small brown dog was seen running about under german wire in front of LES BRIQUES. 3.10pm This was not same dog as reported previously (4-10-15. Daily Diary 2 group.)

F. Rodd
Adj. 2 group

7.38

DAILY DIARY
44th Bde
6-6 pm 9th–10th Oct.

Operations

47th Bk

12.5 , } Registered A 28 b 4½ . ½ .
A.0 pm. } A 28 d 1.5 + AUCHY

57th Bty

Nil.

Information.

Nil.

10.10.15 — Stallard Cptroto
for Lt-Col. R.F.A
Comg 44° Bde

(7·35)

No 22. Anti Aircraft Section

Shooting Report between 7 p.m. to 10.10.15

Time	Objective	Finish	Remarks
3.55 p.m.	German L.V.G.	30.	
5.10 to 5.25 p.m.	3 " L.V.G.	136.	

T. Nestor
Capt. R.N.a
Comdg. 22. A.A. Section

10/10/15

No 220 Anti "Aircraft" Section

Return of Acetylene use on Engages 10.10.15

Hostile Aircraft	Hostile Rounds of Gun	Hostile Rounds of Pistol	Rounds fired from Aircraft Gun	Remarks
Beam	4	20 ANTIDOTUM	5.71 3.65 6 2.30	

T.C. Newton
Lieut. R.40
Comdg. of Aircraft.
Clear & Calm

10/10/15

S E C R E T.   Copy No...4... 1345

2ND DIVISION OPERATION ORDER No. 67.

Reference Maps :-   10th October, 1915.
 BETHUNE Combined Sheet, 1/40,000,
 Trench Map, Sheet 36.c.NW.1, 1/10,000.

    1. Today, 10th October, 5th Infantry Brigade will take over part of the front line as under. All arrangements will be made direct between the Brigade Commanders concerned:-
        From 2nd Guards Brigade (H.Q. at BARTS.)
          From G.4.a.7.4 (LEFT BOYAU exclusive) to the VERMELLES - AUCHY-LEZ-LA-BASSEE road exclusive.
        From 21st Brigade of the 7th Division.
          From AUCHY-LEZ-LA-BASSEE road inclusive to R.1 exclusive.

        Southern Boundary - LEFT BOYAU exclusive - POINT G.3.d.5.8 inclusive - round the "g" of G.3 - east of SUSSEX TRENCH (exclusive) to the railway at GUY'S - thence along the railway.
        Northern Boundary - A line between R and R.1 - then just east of HEADQUARTERS TRENCH - junction of LEWIS ALLEY and HEADQUARTERS TRENCH inclusive - thence North of LEWIS KEEP, leaving LEWIS ALLEY to 2nd Division.

        <u>Communication Trenches</u> - LEWIS ALLEY, RAILWAY ALLEY, GUYS ALLEY

        <u>Keeps to be taken over</u> - LEWIS KEEP, SIM'S KEEP, RAILWAY KEEP.

    5th Infantry Brigade will take over the H.Q. of 21st Inf. Brigade, and will assume command of the line as the relief of each brigade is completed.
    Cottages N.E. of FOSSE 9, F.29.d. are available for billeting reserve battalions of 5th Infantry Brigade.

    2. 1st East Anglian Field Company, R.E. will be affiliated for work to 5th Infantry Brigade. Arrangements for relief of 54th Field Company, R.E. of 7th Division and 76th Field Company, R.E. of Guards Divn. will be made direct between the C.R.E's of Divisions.

    3. Arrangements for artillery support will be notified later.

    4. No.15 Trench Battery will be attached to 5th Infantry Brigade. Application will be made by 5th Inf.Bde. to the A.A. & Q.M.G., 2nd Divn. for necessary transport.

    5. 2nd Division will take over evacuation of the new line under arrangements to be made direct between A.D's.M.S. of Divns.concerned.

    6. Two battalions of 19th Infantry Brigade now at ANNEZIN, VENDIN and OBLINGHEM will move on 10th October to billets in BEUVRY: leading battn.not to reach BEUVRY before 4 p.m.

    7. G.O.C., 2nd Division will assume command of the line taken over on completion of the relief.

    8. 2nd Division report centre unchanged.

                                      Louis Vaughan
                                         Lieut-Colonel,
                                      S.G.S.O., 2nd Division.

Issued at 2 a.m. to :-
    Copy No.1... 5th Inf.Bde.   Copy No.8... A.D.M.S.
     ,,   2... 6th Inf.Bde.   ,,   9... "Q"
     ,,   3... 19th Inf.Bde.   ,, 10... A.P.M.
     ,,   4... R.A.,2nd Div.   ,, 11... 1st Corps.) For
             (att.7th Div)   ,, 12... 7th Divn.   )
     ,,   5... Div.Mtd.Troops.   ,, 13... Guards Divn.) Information
     ,,   6... No.1 Bty.M.M.G.S.   ,, 14-18. G.S. and record.
     ,,   7... 2nd Div. Signals.   ,, 19... R.E., 2nd Divn.

Copy No 8

7TH DIVISION OPERATION ORDER No. 48.

by

Major General H.E.Watts, C.B., C.M.G., Commanding 7th Division.

Divisional Head Qrs.
10th October, 1915.

Following moves will take place today.-

1. The 5th Infantry Brigade of the 2nd Division will take over that portion of the front now held by the 21st Infantry Brigade to R.1. exclusive.

2. The 21st Infantry Brigade will relieve the 20th Infantry Brigade from R.1. inclusive to CAMBRIN - LA BASSEE Road inclusive.

3. The 22nd Infantry Brigade will relieve the 20th Infantry Brigade from their present left to the CAMBRIN - LA BASSEE Road exclusive.

4. Details of the above relief and exact points of junction of the Brigades will be settled between the Brigadiers concerned.

The dividing lines between the 2nd and 7th Divisions will be LEWIS ALLEY, allotted to the 2nd Division.

5. LEWIS KEEP and SIMS KEEP will be handed over to the 2nd Division.

6. Present Headquarters of the 21st Infantry Brigade will be handed over to the 5th Infantry Brigade.

21st Infantry Brigade will establish their Headquarters in the Chemist's Shop, CAMBRIN.

7. The two battalions of the 2nd Division now forming the 7th Divisional reserve will revert to the 2nd Division on completion of the relief.

8/

8.   G.O's C. concerned will assume command of their new areas on completion of the relief, which will be reported to Divisional Headquarters.

9.   The 20th Infantry Brigade will come into Divisional reserve on completion of the relief, in an area which will be communicated to it later.

10.   The 21st Infantry Brigade will retain control of the arrangements for the mortar smoke barrage.

F. Gathorne Hardy
Lieut-Colonel.
General Staff, 7th Division.

Issued at 1030 a.m. to :-

A.D.C. (for G.O.C.)	Copy No. 1.
G.S.O. 1.	" 2.
G.S.O. 2. (Office copy)	" 3.
A.A.&.Q.M.G.	" 4.
7th Signal Company.	" 5.
7th Cyclist Company.	" 6.
Divisional Sqdn. N.H.	" 7.
2nd Divisional Artillery.	" 8.
C.R.E.	" 9.
20th Infantry Brigade.	" 10.
21st Infantry Brigade.	" 11.
22nd Infantry Brigade.	" 12.
A.D.M.S.	" 13.
7th Divisional Train.	" 14.
1st Corps.	" 15.
2nd Division.	" 16.
Guards Division.	" 17.
19th Division.	" 18.

DAILY AMMUNITION RETURN.   10th Oct 1915

Piece	Projectile	Code	\multicolumn{12}{c	}{B A T T E R I E S.}	Total	Per piece
			50	70	15	48	71	9	16	17	47	53	118	3rd(by)div		
2.75	Guns Shrapnel	P														
	H.E.	PX														
18-pr	Guns Shrapnel	A	24	7	-	-	-	4	37	55		73	173		373	
	H.E.	AX	14	119	-	-	-	166	2	90		244	570		1314	
4.5" How.	Howitzers Shrapnel	B						3							3	
	H.E.	EX						8							8	
6" How	Howitzers Shrapnel	H														
	H.E.	F														
	A.P.															

Ams Return.   9 & 10th

"A" Form.
MESSAGES AND SIGNALS.

Army Form C. 2121.

Office of Origin and Service Instructions: Secret

	31	24	41	44 Brigade

TO

Sender's Number	Day of Month	In reply to Number	AAA
B~ 777	10		

Following moves will take place today viz. 5th Infantry Brigade will take over that portion of the front now held by 2nd Guards Brigade and 2nd Infantry Brigade from G.T.q.B.4.1/2 to A.27.d.8.10 — 21st Infantry Brigade will relieve the 2nd Infantry Brigade from A.27.d.8.10 to CAMBRAI — LA BASSÉE road and 22nd Infantry Brigade will take up the front from the road to the canal — C.R.H. support will be provided for 22nd Brigade by 2nd Brigade was for 21st Brigade by 21st Brigade plus Hy. Battery and by 5th Infantry Brigade by 5th Brigade confirm to be notified later aaa Acknowledge

From
Place R.A. 2 Div
Time 11 noon

(777)

Progress Report. 31st Bde R.F.A.

The night was quiet on the front of the 31st Brigade. Continuous rifle fire reported to the South of our zone, and the enemy reported to be firing a lot of flares.

The 103rd Battery fired on transport in HAISNES last night, but owing to considerable firing by our guns, it was difficult to hear what happened; the movement was reported to have ceased after their fire.

Wire cutting is being continued this morning.

Our aeroplanes have just brought down an enemy machine near ANNEQUIN mines, after a 20 minutes battle.

9.0 a.m.
11·10·15

K G Ireland
Capt R.F.A.
for O.C. 31st Brigade R.F.A.

882

Bde Maj. R.A. 2nd Divn – Progress Report

All quiet during the night except for a good deal of rifle fire and flares from the Germans who appeared to be expecting an attack.

At 9.20 pm 103rd Battery fired at transport heard to be moving in HAISNES and reported by the Infantry. HAISNES AVCH.Y.20 was searched.

This morning a German Aviatik was forced to land not far from Bde H.Q. after an exciting chase.

During the day Wire cutting (mentioned in a separate report) and a systematic bombardment of the buildings of FOSSE No 8 was carried out and much damage done. This will be continued tomorrow. A good many of the houses are in ruins but I think some heavy shell are required to give assist in the destruction.

A 5.9 How Battery at 2.35 pm began to shell area South of VERMELLES & continued about 1 rd every 10 minutes for 1½ hours. Direction of fire appeared to come from LA BASSÉE.

11/10/15

J. H. Boyd
Capt. Bde Maj R.A.

— Brigade Major Ragsadin. — 2/883

Wire cutting has been carried out today by the Batteries of this Brigade. Each Battery fired a few Shrapnel to get range and line and then fired 200 rounds H.E. All Batteries report observation of the wire very difficult. though 2 out of 3 BC's observed from support trenches and the other Battery had a forward observing officer. The wire is reported low and much concealed by grass. It is also reported that there are loose coils of wire in front of the parapet. The actual result is difficult to estimate but Observing officers say that it was very often hit. Stakes in some cases were thrown up into the air. Probably about 40% of the rounds hit the front parapet and knocked it about a good deal. A considerable number of rounds seemed to burst after graze. It appeared to me that about 30% behaved in this manner.

The 69th Battery fired at Wire near A 28 c 5.7½ the front of between 50 and 100 yds.
The 103rd Battery fired at A 27 b 9.5 to b 9.3 and at A 28 a 1.1
The 100th Bty fired at A 27 b 10.2 for a distance of 100 yds to South East.

2.

From what I saw of the shooting I would prefer lime Shrapnel with a long corrector but the effect of the fire on the wire may have been quite good. and will be good against enemy wire entanglements with short posts.

H.H. Brady Lt Col RM
Comd 31st Bde RFA

10/10/15

DAILY DIARY.

Z 2 group.   11-10-15

9th Batt fired on HAINES from 6-8 pm
Then they fired on the front trenches
FRANKS KEEP and CORONS de
PEKIN for rest of the day. The earth
parapet of Franks keep was
levelled and the parapet elsewhere
damaged. Two houses in the CORONS
were destroyed.

17th Batt fired on German front trench
wire and parapet only a small
gap was cut in wire. Fired on
CORONS but dust make it impossible
to ascertain damage.

118th Batt fired on German parapet
50x SW of MINE point. about 20x
of parapet here was severly damaged.
Fired also on Houses SW of CORONS
de PEKIN; these houses are now
pretty well demolished but the
debris forms a large mound. The
ground floor may have been
sandbagged.

47th How. Batt. fired on house at A22d 9.6½ suspected of harbouring machine guns; also fired on other houses in A0C4? and points A29c 2.3 and 2.2 A22d 8.8.

GENERAL Effect of H.E. as reported good on parapets but not satisfactory on wire which is merely thrown up and falls back on same place.
 A considerable amount of new earth has been thrown up on HAINES Ridge.
 Germans shelled BACK 8ts and BRAINES way at 9-am about 40 rds.

Rodd Lt.
Adj. 2 group.

(17 / 7.40 pm)

"A" Form.   Army Form C. 2121.

MESSAGES AND SIGNALS.

TO: Ra 2nd DW

Sender's Number: BG/179
Day of Month: 11

AAA

Daily Report A 34th Brigade.
50th Bty fired on EMBANKMENT REDOUBT between 10 & 11 am in retaliation and again at 4pm.
70th Bty retaliated at 10.55 am 12.10 & 2.20 pm on enemy's trenches. Registered No.3 gun at 3pm.

Observation possible 6.30 – 8.30 am. Several enemy aeroplanes seen on our front, one of which was brought down near Fosse no 9. Our front very quiet except for a little pipsqueaking.

Childard
Capt.

1G
7.40pm

	"A" Form.			Army Form C. 2121.	
	MESSAGES AND SIGNALS.			No. of Message	
Prefix Code m.	Words	Charge	This message is on a/c of:	Recd. at m.	
Office of Origin and Service Instructions.	Sent			Date	
	At m.		Service.	From	
	To			By	
	By		(Signature of "Franking Officer.")		

TO: **Ra 2nd Div.**

Sent Number.	Day of Month. 11	In reply to Number	AAA

Report on wire cutting.

50th Bty.
About 120 rounds fired mostly H.E. Front 20 yards. Very few stakes left standing and very little uncut wire; but there is a lot of wire bundled which is not swept away. H.E. was good for uprooting stakes but did not sweep away the wire. The rounds on the trenches did a lot of damage to the parapet.

70th Bty.
About 110 rounds H.E. fired on front trench & wire just North of main Road. Effect on parapet excellent, very little being left above ground level.

From
Place
Time

The above may be forwarded as now corrected. (Z)

Censor. Signature of Addressor or person authorised to telegraph in his name.
* This line should be erased if not required.

"A" Form.
Army Form C. 2121.

MESSAGES AND SIGNALS.

The wire is in 2 if not 3 lines, the front being loose rolls & the others on stakes about 4 ft. high. The rolls were cut in 3 places each about 6 ft wide. The staked wire was damaged but there was only one real gap.

Effect of H.E on wire appears extremely local and has the effect of making the whole entanglement sink, instead of blowing it into the air (probably owing to the fact of the very high velocity of the fragments as they cut the strands) O.C. considers that H.E. compares unfavourably with shrapnel for this purpose.

Ammn 70th Bty

About 10% Blinds - (partly soft ground) Several detonated indifferently

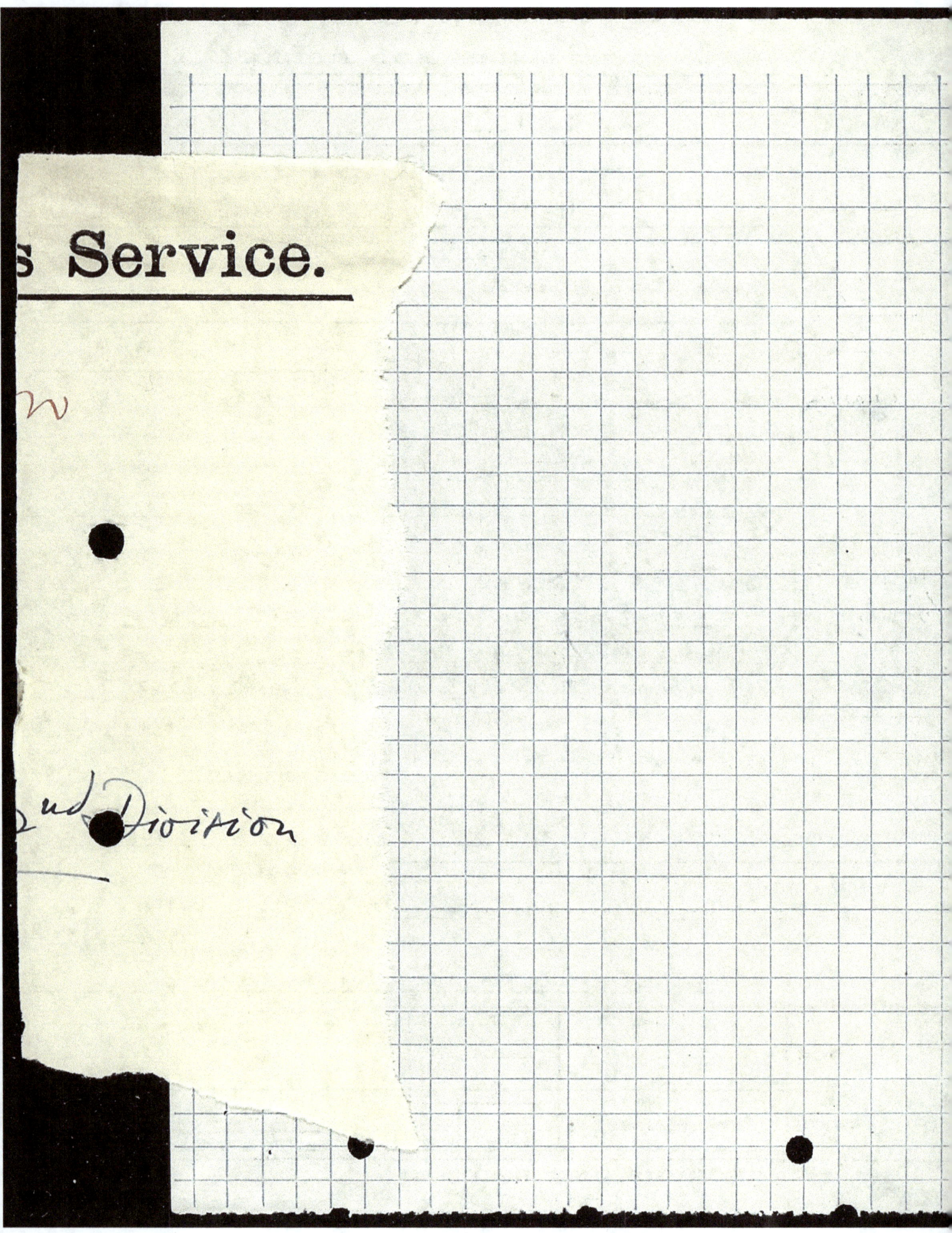

"A" Form.
Army Form C. 2121.
MESSAGES AND SIGNALS.

Prefix	Code	m.	Words	Charge	This message is on a/c of:	Recd. at	m.
Office of Origin and Service Instructions.			Sent			Date	
			At	m.	Service.	From	
			To			By	
			By		(Signature of "Franking Officer.")		

TO {

Sender's Number.	Day of Month.	In reply to Number	**AAA**

Certain number appear to burst in air about 15 ft from ground (possibly ricochet and delayed action of fuze)

One round evidently exploded some bombs in enemy front trench as a violent explosion occurred after shell had detonated & there were showers of sparks & smoke.

Childard
Capt.

From
Place
Time

The above may be forwarded as now corrected. (Z)

Censor. Signature of Addressor or person authorised to telegraph in his name.

* This line should be erased if not required.

DAILY DIARY.
44th Bde.
6—6 pm. 10th – 11th Oct.

Operations.

47th Bty.
11.30 am. Fired at house A 22 d 9.6½.
suspected of containing machine guns.

11.45 am } Registration on A 29 c 2.3
1.20 pm.   } A 29 c 2.2   A 22 d 8.8   and
4.30 pm.   } other houses in AUCHY.

56th Bty
2.10 pm. Registered RAILWAY REDOUBT.

Information
Nil.

H Welch Capt. L. BC. R.F.A
Comdg. 44th Bde.

	A.M.	P.M.
Arrives Plain B.C. select Colors		
	8/-	2/6
	10.30	4.15

ARNEQUIN
30.
7.
13.

T.D.Newton

11/10/15

22 Anti Aircraft Station
Shooting Report   5 Y. Pm   11·10 – 15ᵐ

Time	Objective	Rds fired	Remarks
8.55 Am	German L.O.G	28	*Brought down
9.0 "	observations	25	British planes near
9.45 "	German L.O.G	60	SAILLY-LABOURSE.
10.0 "	"	44	
10.15 "	"	31	
3.20 Pm	"	45	
4.0 "	"	43	

T.C.Newton
Capt R.H.A
Cmdg. 22. A.A. Station.

11/10/15

"A" Form. Army Form C. 2121.
MESSAGES AND SIGNALS.

Office of Origin and Service Instructions: Secret

TO: 34th Bde / 44th Bde / MEERUT RA

Sender's Number: M 782
Day of Month: 10

In the event of the call COOPERATE IND ONE being received by 34th Bde they will direct fire on TOWPATH ALLEY and PLAIN ALLEY and will also inform 56th Battery who will fire on works A11C1.4 and 17a central aaa Fire to be at a steady rate and to be carried on pending further ~~Sugar~~ information as to situation aaa Addressed 34th and 44th repeated MEERUT aaa

From: RA 7 Div.
Time: 6.35 pm

J Mowbray Major

Secret

C R A II Division

The G.O.C Meerut Division has asked me to arrange with you for artillery support in the event of it being needed, on that portion of the German front extending from A9a 67 to A9d 57

Would you kindly inform me at your earliest convenience what 18 P^{rs} and 4.5" Howitzer fire you can bring to bear on the front line, support and communication trenches of the front above mentioned.

Should you be unable to bring any fire to bear from existing positions, would you please say what arrangements you will take to carry this into effect, and when it may be counted.

The G.O.C considers this arrangement to be absolutely necessary.

If one battery 18 P^{rs} & one section of Howitzers could be switched on to this area, it should suffice for the purpose.

If you will kindly inform me of the position of the supporting guns, I will arrange what trenches they should register on.

L.A.Gordon
Brig Genl
C R A Meerut Divn

10th Octr 15

"A" Form.
MESSAGES AND SIGNALS.
Army Form C. 2121.

Secret

TO RA MEERUT Div.

Sender's Number: Bm 783
Day of Month: 11
In reply to Number: G1
AAA

We can at any time bring unaimed fire of one 18 pr. battery and one section 5in. howitzers to bear on CANTELEUX & CANTELEUX ALLEY N & S as far west as A10a&C 0.0 aaa In addition we can give you a position about F18C from which to fire on that area or anywhere else in our area which you may select aaa We do not see how we can undertake the close and immediate work necessary to meet an emergency situation without devoting guns with observers specially for the purpose aaa

From
Place
Time 783   12-45p

(Z) H Andrews Brig Genl
C R A 9 Div

Motor Cycle

DAILY AMMUNITION RETURN.   11th Oct 1915.

Piece	Projectile	Code	50	70	15	48	71	9	16	17	47	53	31Bd	11Bd	Total	Per piece
2.75	Guns Shrapnel	P														
	H.E.	PX														
18-pr	Guns Shrapnel	A	66	6	-	-	28	73	4	-	90	-			267	
	H.E.	AX	107	58	-	-	49	14	-	214	-	1351	314		2567	
4.5" How.	Howitzers Shrapnel	B							2	-					2	
	H.E.	EX							52	51					103	
6" How	Howitzers Shrapnel	H														
	H.E.	F														
	A.P.															

2nd Divisional Artillery Orders

By

Brig.Genl. G.H.Sanders, D.S.O. C.R.A.2nd Divn.

11th October, 1915.

1036. Traffic.

No horse drawn vehicle is to proceed at a pace faster than a walk on the BEUVRY-LA BASSEE road to the east of the cross road in F.29.b.

Disciplinary action will be taken against any person in charge of vehicles contravening this order.

1037. Inspection of Drafts.

When men of drafts joining units of the Division are considered by the O.C. the unit or the Medical Officer to be of inferior quality, a notification will be made to the A.D.M.S. of the Division who will arrange for the early inspection of the men concerned.

1038. Equipment.

All condemned running out springs from 60-pr, 4.7", 18-pr or 13-pr. guns and 4.5" howitzers, should be collected if possible and sent to the Base for transmission to Woolwich.
O.S.11/152. 1st Army, 8th October 1915.

1039. Discipline.

Several cases have occurred of late in which Officers Commanding Batteries have summarily dealt with offences which should have been referred to Superior Authority.

Attention is directed to the provisions of paragraph 487 King's Regulations and Section 106 Field Service Regulations Part II.

L. G. Buxton   Captain R.A.

Staff Captain R. A. 2nd Division.

DAILY DIARY

2a group.   12-10-15

9th Batt fired on CORONS DE PEKIN from 10.30 am till 11 am and from 2.30 pm onwards, destroying several houses. At 11 am shelled german parapet where it had been repaired and also FRANKS KEEP.

17th Batt fired on CORONS de PEKIN; and front german parapet making several clear breaches where you were able to see right through.

118th Batt. fired on CORONS de PEKIN and german front trenches. Retaliated during last night for bombing near mine point.

47th Batt fired on A28 B O.8

GENERAL The houses in the CORONS are now so demolished that further shooting does not have so much effect, the debris forming large heaps. Germans shelled our trenches A21C and D from direction of HAINES at 12 noon with 77 mm and 4.2 at 5.15pm they shelled trenches W. of

HOHENZOLLERN
A new trench has been dug down the HAINES ridge from about A30c 6-9 towards 29d 5.4
A lot of new wire has been put up round CEMETARY
lights as reported were thrown up this evening

Rodd Lt
Adj. Z.2 group.

(13)
7.30/p.

"A" Form.
MESSAGES AND SIGNALS.
Army Form C. 2121.

TO	Ra 2nd DW

Sender's Number.	Day of Month.	In reply to Number.	AAA
BG/180	12		

Daily Report 34th Brigade

50th Bty.

Fired at intervals during the night on EMBANKMENT REDOUBT and FALSE CULVERT. 9am today fired at snipers on North face of EMBANKMENT REDOUBT with good effect on parapet as well as snipers. Cut wire 11am - 12noon. Shot at sniper North of CANAL at 2.30pm.

70th Bty.

Today 12.30pm retaliated on trenches to enemy shelling.

3.45pm on wire and parapet.

Observation possible 7am - 8am. Misty early - Light very good from 9am. Our front all quiet.

Geldard
Capt

"A" Form.
MESSAGES AND SIGNALS.
Army Form C. 2121.

TO: Ra 2nd DW.

Day of Month: 12.
AAA

Wire cutting.
Both batteries reports are similar. All stakes have disappeared. The wire is thrown into the air by the shell fire but seems to drop back again, and although probably broken to pieces remains bunched up. H.E. does not clear a way right through the wire although it is probably surmountable in many places. Effect on parapet very good.

Childard
Capt. for
cmdg 34th Bde R.F.A.

From: 13
Place:
Time: 7.30 pm

DAILY DIARY
44th Bde.
6-6 pm. 11th-12th Oct

Operations.
47th Bty.
4.30 pm. Fired one round at A.28.b.0.8.

56th Bty.
11.55 pm. Fired on MINNENWERFER at A.22.a.0.9½
at request of infantry.
1.45 pm. Fired on MINNENWERFER at A.22.a.0.9½
at request of infantry.

Information.
11.50 am to 12 noon. Hostile shelling on
trenches in A.21.d & A.21.c. 4.2" & 77 mm
from direction of HAISNES.
5.15 pm. 4.2" shelled trenches W of
HOHENZOLLERN REDOUBT.

E.A. Harpur B-Cr R.F.A.
Comdg. 44th Bde.

12.10.15

No 22. Anti- Aircraft Section

Returns of Aeroplanes seen Engaged

Hostile Planes		Allied Planes	Position of Battery	Hostile Planes Shot active believers		Remarks
Seen	Engaged	Seen		A.M.	P.M.	
5	3.	24	ANNEQUIN	—	3.25 pm to 6.30.	

T C Newton Capt. R.H.A.
Comdg. 22. A.A. Section

105

No. 22 Anti Aircraft Section   113

Shooting Report   to Y.P.M. 13.10.15

Time	Objective	Rds fired	Remarks
5.25.pm	2 German A.V.C.	40.	
6.25 "	1 " " "	75	

T C Newton Capt. R.H.A
Comdg 22. A.A. Section

SECRET.

2nd Divn. No.
G.S.657/5.

1354

5th Infantry Brigade.
46th Division.   )
Guards Division.) For information.
1st Corps.   )

RA 2nd Div

1. The attack of the 11th Corps has been provisionally fixed for 13th October. The left flank of this attack is as indicated to you in my L.V.44 of 10th October.

The line which 46th Division on your right intends to establish includes G.5.b.6.8 - A.29.d.2.5 - N.W. corner of CARONS DE MARON - A.29.c.1.6 - A.28.d.4.9 and along AUCHY - VERMELLES Road to our present front trench A.28.c.3.3.

The programme for the preparation of the attack has already been issued to you with my L.V.40, dated 10th October, and you will work on the assumption that this programme will come into force at 1 p.m. on 13th October, and that the assault will take place at 2 p.m. that day. These hours have been fixed provisionally. Exact timings will be notified later.

All your arrangements must be complete by 1 p.m. on 13th.

2. The part to be played by your brigade in this attack consists of :-

(a). A curtain of smoke from the trenches to be made with smoke grenades. The detail of this is as communicated to you in 2nd Division No. G.S.567/2 of 10th October, amended by my L.V.43 of same date.

Arrangements will be made for 21 Groups. Each of these Groups will discharge 45 smoke grenades, in accordance with instructions already issued, and will also discharge 5 extra grenades *and 5 Smoke Candles* during the last ten minutes, in order to thicken up the smoke. "Q" will now issue to you an extra 105 grenades, *and 105 Candles* (5 per group) for this purpose.

(b)

(2)

(b). <u>Machine Gun Fire</u> - This consists of 2 separate schemes.

(i). Scheme notified in 2nd Division No.G.S.657/1 of 10th October. This occupied 8 machine guns. Fire from these machine guns will be opened on the date of attack between the hours of 1 p.m. and 2 p.m. All fire from these guns to cease at 2 p.m.

^xScheme attached -

(ii). Machine Gun Fire for which you are at present making a^xscheme, as directed in my L.V.44 of 10th October. To the targets therein given you will add MADAGASCAR TRENCH.

The targets to be engaged in this scheme will therefore be :-
LITTLE WILLIE,
FOSSE TRENCH,
MAD POINT,
MADAGASCAR,
MADAGASCAR TRENCH and
enfilade fire on the VERMELLES - AUCHY road.

Your attention is again drawn to the necessity of stopping all machine gun fire south of MAD POINT - MADAGASCAR and PEKIN ALLEY at 2 p.m., when the assault takes place. Fire will however be continued on the targets mentioned north of this line after that hour, by any machine guns whose lines are clear of the line of assault.

(c). <u>Smoke Barrage on MAD POINT</u>. The object is to put a smoke barrage between MAD POINT - MADAGASCAR, and the assaulting troops. For this, 2 Groups of smoke-producing mortars are available, viz :-

<u>1st Group</u> - From Guards Division - No.64 Trench Battery, (Two 2" mortars) under Lieut.Brassett, R.F.A. and

No.12 Trench Battery (four 1½" mortars) under Lieut.Kyle, R.F.A.

Of these, No.12 Battery fires a man-killing projectile and No.64 Battery fires smoke.

<u>2nd Group</u> - From 7th Division. ~~Under charge of Lieut. Moyer.~~ No.10 Trench Battery (Four 2" mortars) under Lieut Corrie, and 4 95 m.m. mortars under Lieut Battiscombe. All these are for smoke-producing.

Of these, 1st Group will be in action South of the

VERMELLES

(3).

VERMELLES - AUCHY Road and the 2nd Group North of that road.

The detailed procedure to be followed by these batteries will be decided at the conference with the mortar officers summoned at 9 a.m. tomorrow at your Headquarters.

(d). <u>A bomb attack</u> up NEW TRENCH to assist the operations of 46th Division. Detailed instructions on this point will be given to you later, after G.O.C. has discussed the subject with you.

(e). <u>Start a Communication Trench</u> out towards MAD POINT at once by sapping forward on the South side of the VERMELLES - AUCHY Road.

3. A staff officer will visit your Headquarters at on 13th October to give you the official time.

4. In order to give 46th Division more room for forming up, the dividing line between 2nd and 46th Division will, from tomorrow night, be drawn from G.4.a.7.4 to G.4.a.4.5 and thence so as to give RESERVE TRENCH and RAILWAY RESERVE TRENCH to 46th Division. "RESERVE" and "RAILWAY RESERVE" Trenches will be cleared by 2nd Division by <u>9 p.m. 12th October.</u>

RAILWAY ALLEY remains in 2nd Division area.

<u>Issued at 3.0 pm.</u>

Louis Vaughan

2nd Division.
11th October, 1915.

Lieut-Colonel,
S.G.S.O., 2nd Division.

4.5" Hows (2nd, 7th, 28th, Meerut Divs)

Serial No.	How: or Gun.		Targets.			Remarks.
	Nature	No.	12 to 1 pm	1 pm to 2 pm	2 pm onwards	
1	4.5 How:	2 Battys.	LITTLE WILLIE	(a) MAD Point (b) MADAGAS-CAR. ✱ (Lachrymatory)	(a) MAD Point (b) MADAGAS-CAR. (Lachrymatory)	
2.	"	1 "	Trench A28d2.5 - 4½.7½.	Railway redoubt A27b.10.1	as between 1pm & 2pm	2nd
3.	"	1 "	A28d4½.7½ - 8½.6	AUCHY & front row FOSSE COTTAGES ✱ (Lachrymatory)	AUCHY (lyddite)	✱ Auchy 1pm to 1.45pm
4.	"	1 "	A28d8½.6 - 4½.2.	AUCHY.	as between 1pm & 2pm	2nd
5.	"	1 "	FOSSE support Trench.	LES BRIQUES Trench & farm.	"	
6.	"	2 "	SLAG ALLEY.	Under orders of GOC RA. XII" Divn		
7.	"	1 "	1 gun Cemetery Alley. 2 guns on Canal Alley.	As in (1)	As in (1)	

✱ Lachrymatory shell between 1.45pm & 2pm

2nd Divisional Artillery

Serial No.	Gun or How: Nature	No: of Batts.	Targets. 12 to 2 p.m. *	2 p.m. to 2.15 p.m.	2.15 p.m. onwards
1.	18-pdr.	2	Area enclosed as follows:- A29c1.6 - along W.edge of CORONS DE MARON-thence along N.E.edge of CORONS DE PEKIN just S.of 3 CABARETS to A26d25-A29d22- A29d20-thence along N.E. side of DUMP.	As in (1)	A23d.42. to A24c10.0.
2.	"	2			A29b48 to A30a8.8
3.	"	1			A22d84 to A29a2.8½

* Shrapnel only from 1 p.m. to 2.15 p.m.

SECRET.

C.R.A.
2nd Div Arty

The XI th Corps will attack the enemy tomorrow (13th October). The bombardment of the enemy's positions by all Guns of the Corps will commence at 12 noon.

At 2.0 p.m. the Infantry assault will be launched. Acknowledge.

R.C.Rome.

12th October. 1915.
              Captain.
             Staff Officer
             R.A XIth Corps.

Rept to:
1st H.A.R.
5th — —
Siege Group
28th Div Arty Group
Meerut Div Arty
XII Div Arty Group

SECRET.   Copy No. 4

2ND DIVISION OPERATION ORDER No. 68.

Reference Trench Map, 36.c.NW,   12th October, 1915.
Sheets 1 & 3, 1/10,000.

1. In order to establish a defensive flank with a view to a further advance South of the LA BASSEE Canal, 11th Corps are tomorrow attacking the QUARRIES and FOSSE No.8 and intend to connect their left with our trenches about VERMELLES - AUCHY Road.

46th Division is attacking FOSSE No.8.
The 138th Infantry Brigade on the left of 46th Division, is attacking from our front trenches between G.4.d.2.6 and G.4.a.7.2.
The assault takes place at 2 p.m. tomorrow, 13th October.

<u>1st Objective</u> - A.29.c.5.3 exclusive to A.29.c.1.6 - A.28.d.8.3 and 4.3 - 1st "L" of LITTLE WILLIE to our present front trench at A.28.c.5.1.

Bombing parties are following the assault, to bomb along the following trenches :-
  (i). Trench leading N.W. from N.W. face of HOHENZOLLERN REDOUBT.
  (ii). LITTLE WILLIE.
  (iii). FOSSE TRENCH.

<u>2nd Objective</u> - A.29.a.3.0 - A.28.d.8.8 - A.28.b.4.1 - A.28.d.4.9 - MAD POINT - Front trench at A.28.c.3.3.

The 2nd objective is the line which 46th Division intends to establish.

During the assault a barrage is being formed, which will continue on MAD POINT and MADAGASCAR from 2 to 4 p.m., after which it is to be lifted to AUCHY ALLEY.

If the wind is favourable, the assault will be preceded by smoke and gas from 1 to 2 p.m.

1st Corps is co-operating in the discharge of smoke and gas.
North of the Canal the Indian and 3rd Corps are carrying out a demonstration.

After 2 p.m., if the gas has been effective, 7th Division are sending out demolition parties to destroy the enemy's mine plant in their front trenches.

2. 5th Infantry Brigade will :-
  (i). Start gas and smoke curtain from their trenches at 1 p.m.
  (ii). Form a smoke barrage on MAD POINT with trench mortars at 1 p.m.
  (iii). Open machine gun fire.

Instructions and time tables for the execution of these tasks have been issued separately to 5th Infantry Brigade.
5th Infantry Brigade will also at 2 p.m., carry out a bomb attack up NEW TRENCH to co-operate with the bombing parties of the 46th Division. Instructions for this attack have been issued separately.

3. All troops, 2nd Division (less 5th Infantry Brigade and affiliated troops holding the line) will be prepared to move at 2 hours notice if required from 2 p.m. tomorrow.

(2)

4. The following distinguishing flags are being used :-

46th Division :-
To mark the position of infantry in the firing line.) 3' square screens divided diagonally into red and yellow.

To mark position of bombing parties in captured trenches.) Red flag 18" square.

2nd Division :-
To mark the position of bombing parties in captured trenches.) Yellow flags 18" square.

Men raising caps on bayonets will also be used to denote the position gained by 2nd Division bombers.

7th Division :-
To mark position of demolition parties.) Screens red & blue diagonally one side, khaki reverse side.

5. Watches will be set by signal time sent out by Corps Signals at 9 a.m., 13th instant.

6. 2nd Division report centre unchanged.

[signature]

Lieut-Colonel,
S.G.S.O., 2nd Division.

Issued at 9 p.m. to:-
```
Copy No.1...... 5th Infantry Brigade.
 ,,    2...... 6th Infantry Brigade.
 ,,    3...... 19th Infantry Brigade.
 ,,    4...... R.A., 2nd Division.
 ,,    5...... R.E., 2nd Division.
 ,,    6...... Divisional Mounted Troops.
 ,,    7...... No.1 Bty. H.M.G.Service.
 ,,    8...... Divisional Signal Co.
 ,,    9...... A.D.M.S.
 ,,   10...... A.P.M.
 ,,   11...... "Q".
 ,,   12...... O.C., Train.
 ,,   13...... 1st Corps.              )
 ,,   14...... Adv. 46th Division.     ) For information.
 ,,   15...... Adv. 7th Division.      )
 ,, Nos.16-20. G.S. and Record.
```

S E C R E T. Copy No. 8

7TH DIVISION OPERATION ORDER No. 49.
by
Major-General H. E. Watts, C.B., C.M.G.,
Commanding, 7th Division.

Reference Trench Map 1/10,000.

October 12th, 1915.

1. The XIth Corps will tomorrow attack and capture the QUARRIES and FOSSE No. 8, connecting with our present system of trenches about the VERMELLES - AUCHY Road.
   The attack on the QUARRIES will be carried out by the 12th Division, that on FOSSE No. 8 by the 46th Division. The 138th Infantry Brigade will be the left Brigade of the 46th Division, and will attack with its left from G.4.a.7.2. directed on to A.29.c.1.6.
   Bombing parties will follow the assault and bomb along LITTLE WILLIE and FOSSE TRENCH, with the object of gaining MAD POINT.
   2nd Division will bomb up NEW TRENCH in co-operation with the 46th Division bombing parties.
   The Indian Corps, North of the Canal, will demonstrate with smoke.

2. The 7th Division will co-operate in this attack by a gas and smoke attack, if the wind proves favourable, and with Machine gun fire.

3. The hour of zero has been fixed for 1.p.m. Timetable for gas attack will be as under :-

1.p.m. to 1-50.p.m.	Gas and Smoke.	Start the gas and smoke simultaneously. At the commencement turn on two cylinders per bay at the same time, then reduce to one cylinder per bay, and finish up with two cylinders per bay.
1-50.p.m. to 2.p.m.	Smoke.	Turn off gas at 1-50.p.m. and thicken up smoke by using extra candles, grenades etc.
2.p.m.	Assault.	

4. 21st Infantry Brigade will establish two guns in KINGSWAY to fire on MADAGASCAR TRENCH from 1.p.m. to 2.p.m.
   Two guns in RUSSELL KEEP to fire on LES BRIQUES and RAILWAY WORK, at intervals, from 1.p.m. to 4.p.m.
   Two guns in the Support Trench between BOYAU 7 and 8 to fire on AUCHY ALLEY, at intervals, between 1.p.m. and 4.p.m.

The/

The remainder of the Machine guns of the 21st and 22nd Infantry Brigades will fire on the hostile front and communication trenches from 1.p.m. onwards, under arrangements to be made by G.O's C. Brigades concerned.

5. No. 10. Mortar battery will form a smoke barrage under orders which have been issued by the 2nd Division.

6. At the end of the gas attack, the 21st and 22nd Infantry Brigades will, if there seems any likelihood of the enemy having been completely driven from their trenches, send forward patrols to examine them and collect all possible information.

7. The Artillery covering our front will keep the hostile front trenches under Artillery fire between 1. and 2.p.m. At 2.p.m. they will lift 200 yards so as to allow the advance of the patrols.

8. The following distinguishing flags will be used :-

<u>46th Division.</u>

To mark the position of infantry in the firing line.	3' square screens divided diagonally into red and yellow.
To mark position of bombing parties in captured trenches.	Red flag 18" square.

<u>2nd Division.</u>

To mark the position of bombing parties in captured trenches.	Yellow screens, reverse side khaki.

Men raising caps on bayonets will also be used to denote the position gained by the 2nd Division bombers.

9. Watches will be set by Signal time at 9.a.m. tomorrow morning.

10. Divisional Headquarters will remain at LE QUESNOY.

F. Gathorne Hardy
Lieut-Colonel.
<u>General Staff, 7th Division.</u>

Issued/

Issued at 8.45 p.m. to :-

    A.D.C. (for G.O.C.)   Copy No. 1.
    G.S.O. 1.   " 2.
    G.S.O. 2 (Office copy)   " 3.
    A.A.&Q.M.G.   " 4.
    7th Signal Company.   " 5.
    7th Cyclist Company.   " 6.
    Divisional Sqdn. N.H.   " 7.
    2nd Divisional Artillery.   " 8.
    C.R.E.   " 9.
    20th Infantry Brigade.   " 10.
    21st Infantry Brigade.   " 11.
    22nd Infantry Brigade.   " 12.
    A.D.M.S.   " 13.
    7th Divisional Train.   " 14.
    1st Corps.   " 15.
    2nd Division.   " 16.
    Meerut Division.   " 17.
    170th Mining Company, R.E.   " 18.
    173rd Mining Company, R.E.   " 19.
    Captain. Berrisford.   " 20.

S E C R E T.

~~20th~~)
21st) ~~Infantry Brigade.~~
~~22nd~~)
2nd Division R.A.
~~O. R. E.~~
~~Captain Bazzinford.~~

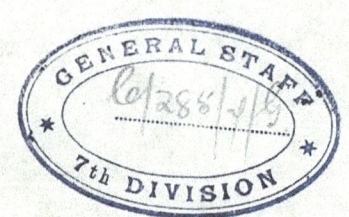

1.   The 12th Division will on October 13th attack the QUARRIES and the 46th Division HOHENZOLLERN REDOUBT, FOSSE No 8, and CORONS DE MAROC. The assault will be made at 0-60.

The hour of zero will in all probability be 1.p.m. but further instructions will be issued on this subject.

2.   This attack will be preceded by a prolonged bombardment, which has already commenced, and by a gas attack in accordance with the time-table issued with this Office No. C/285/3.G. of yesterday's date.

3.   By 6-30. a.m. on October 13th the Division will be concentrated as follows :-

21st Infantry Brigade and 54th Field Company, R.E., in its present system of trenches East of and exclusive of BRADDELL TRENCH.

22nd Infantry Brigade and 2nd Highland Field Company, R.E., in its present system of trenches East of and exclusive of WILLOW LANE.

The garrisons of the various keeps and supporting points should rejoin their units, but in the event of no advance being made these posts should at once be re-occupied.

20th Infantry Brigade in Divisional reserve, one battalion in each of BRADDELL TRENCH and WILLOW LANE, three battalions in the neighbourhood of BEUVRY and LE PREOL. The last three named battalions need not be at their rendezvous until the hour of zero.

95th Field Company, R.E., in Divisional reserve at CAMBRIN Supporting Point.

Brigade Headquarters will be established as follows :-
21st Infantry Brigade.. MAISON ROUGE.
22nd Infantry Brigade.. SIDING 6.
20th Infantry Brigade.. Chemist's Shop, CAMBRIN.

4. On the completion of the gas attack the 21st and 22nd Infantry Brigades will push forward patrols along the whole front and ascertain whether the German front trench is occupied or not. In the event of the Germans being overwhelmed in their front trench, this trench will be at once occupied and consolidated. The 21st Infantry Brigade being responsible for the front from the VERMELLES - LA BASSEE Railway (inclusive) to the CAMBRIN - LA BASSEE Road (inclusive). The 22nd Infantry Brigade for the front from the CAMBRIN - LA BASSEE Road (exclusive) to the CANAL.

5. It is not intended that the attack should be pushed forward further than the German front trench, but bombing and Infantry covering parties should be pushed to the front, whilst this trench is being consolidated.

6. Every communication trench leading into the German front trench from the German rear defences should be completely filled in for a length of at least 50 yards.

Certain previously selected places should be made into keeps in the German line.

7. For the carrying out of the above plan, definite parties must be previously told off and provided with the necessary tools, sandbags, etc.

It is believed that the 2nd Division are carrying

out/

out a similar operation South of the VERMELLES - LA BASSEE Railway. More detailed instructions will be issued on receipt of 1st Corps orders.

F. Gathorne Hardy
Lieut-Colonel.

Divl Hd Qrs.
11th October, 1915.

General Staff, 7th Division.

S E C R E T.

20th)
~~21st~~) ~~Infantry Brigade.~~
~~22nd~~)
2nd Division R.A.
~~C. R. E.~~
~~Captain Berrisford.~~

1. The advance of the 7th Division foreshadowed in this Office No. C/285/7.G. of yesterday's date will not take place. The paper above referred to is therefore cancelled.

2. The gas and smoke attack laid down in this Office No. C/285/5.G. will be carried out as laid down in that paper in conjunction with the advance of the XI Corps.

3. In addition to the Machine guns told off for special tasks in this Office No. C/285/5.G. the Machine guns of the 21st and 22nd Infantry Brigades will keep the hostile front line trenches and communication trenches on their immediate front under fire from 0 onwards.

4. During the working of the gas and smoke attack all emplacements which contain cylinders will be kept clear of all men except those who are absolutely necessary. Two men per emplacement should, under arrangements with the 186th and 188th Companies, R.E., be instructed in the working of the cylinders so that in the event of the R.E. suffering casualties they may be able to continue the necessary work. This instruction will be carried out on the morning of the 13th.

5. The Defensive scheme outlined in this Officer No. 907/G of the 7th inst. will now be pushed forward with all speed.

Divl Hd Qrs.   Lieut-Colonel.
12th October, 1915.
                                        General Staff, 7th Division.

S E C R E T.

2nd Division Artillery Operation Order No.6.

October 12th, 1915.

Reference 1/10,000.
Trench Map.

INFORMATION. 1. The XIth Corps is to attack and capture the QUARRIES (12th Division) and FOSSE NO.8 (46th Division) in order to establish the left flank of the 1st Army and render a further advance, in conjunction with the French, possible.
The line to be established is G 12d 3.9 - G 12b 2.2 - G 6c 8.2 and 4.5 - G 6a 4.2 - A 29d 2.5 - N.W.Corner of CORONS DE MARONS - A 29c 1.6 - A 28d 4.9 and along AUCHY-VERMELLES Road to our present front trench A 28c 3.3.
The attack will take place on the 13th instant. The infantry will assault at 2 hours after zero.

HOUR OF ATTACK. 2. The hour of zero will be notified later.

ARTILLERY SUPPORT. 3. 2nd Division Artillery will co-operate by wire-cutting and destruction of parapets, especially machine gun emplacements, flanking the attack during the morning of the 12th, keeping economy of ammunition in view. And by the following bombardment:-

18 Pounders.

Time.	Unit.	Target.	Remarks.
0-0 to 2-10.	9th Battery. 17th " 103rd " 118th " 69th "	Houses and trenches in area A 28b 5.0.- A 29b 2.0.- G 5b 2.0.- A 29c 7.3.- A 29c 6.2.- A 28b 5.0.	No H.E. after 1-0.
2-10 onwards.	103rd Battery) 70th ")	Road A 29b 9.8 - A 30a 8.8.	
	17th Battery) 48th ")	Trench A 23d 4.2 - A 24c 8.1. (HAISNES ALLEY)	
	100th Battery.	Road A 22d 8.9 - A 29d 3.9.	

4.5" Howitzers.

0-0 to 1-0. 1-0 to 2-0. 2-0 to 2-30. 2-30 onwards.	47th Battery.	Trench A 28d 1.5 - A 28d 5.8. AUCHY CENTRAL. As from 0-0 to 1-0. Trench A 28c 4.8. to A 28a 9.7.	
0-0 to 1-0 1-0 onwards.	56th Battery.	Trench A 28d 5.8 - A 28d 9.6. Railway work.	

From 0-00 to 2-0 batteries not detailed for bombardment will keep up a slow fire on their own front. At 2-10 they will stop and await orders.

S E C R E T.

RATES OF FIRE. 4. Ammunition is allotted as follows:-

<u>18 Pdrs.</u>- 0-0 to 1-0 -   60 rounds per gun.
1-0 to 2-10 -   20 rounds per gun.
2-10 to 4-0 -   50 rounds per gun.
At least 50% H.E. on the day.

<u>4.5" Howitzers.</u>
0-0 to 1-0 -   20 rounds per gun.
1-0 to 2-0 -   AUCHY 10 rounds per gun.
2-0 to 2-30 -   Trench 100 rounds.
2-30 onwards-   Trench 100 rounds.
1-0 onwards -   RAILWAY WORK 300 rounds.

DISTINGUISHING
FLAGS.   5.   <u>46th Division,Infantry.</u>
3' Square Screens divided diagonally into red and yellow.
<u>Bombing parties.</u>-
Red flags 18" square.

Major, R.A.,

Brigade Major, R.A., 2nd Divn.

Issued at........to:-
Copy No.1. 31st F.A.Brigade.
"   2. 34th   "   "
"   3. 41st   "   "
"   4. 44th   "   "
"   5. D.A.C.
"   6. 2nd Division.)
"   7. 7th Division.) For information.
"   8. R.A.,1st Corps)
"   9. RA XI Corps)
"   10. RA 28th Divn.)

36th 18th

Tomorrow morning and up to the hour of zero cut wire at Embankment redoubt and just S. of it sufficiently seriously to make the enemy think an attack is coming there.

S E C R E T.

CORRIGENDA
to
2nd Division Artillery Operation Order No.6.

13th October, 1915.

Add new para. 1a.-
"Both 2nd and 7th Divisions will co-operate in the operations with a gas and smoke attack at 1-0 if the wind prove favourable.

2nd Division will at 2-0 carry out a bomb attack up NEW TRENCH to co-operate with the bombing parties of the 46th Division.

7th Division will at the end of the gas attack, if there seems any likelihood of the enemy having been completely driven from their trenches, send forward patrols to examine them and collect all possible information."

Para.3.18 Pdr table. - for " G 5b 2.0" read "G 5b 2.10" after "on their own front" add "quickening at 1-0 to a steady rate. At 2-0 this fire will lift 200 yards. No H.E. after 1 p.m.".

Para 5 add -
"2nd Division bombing parties -
Yellow screens with reversed side Khaki.
Men raising caps on bayonets.
7th Division patrols -
Screens red and blue diagonally, Khaki reversed side."

Major, R.A.,
Brigade Major, R.A., 2nd Divn.

Issued to:-
31st F.A.Brigade.
34th   "   "
41st   "   "
44th   "   "
D.A.C.
2nd Division.
7th Division.
R.A., 1st Corps.
R.A., XI th Corps.
R.A., 28th Division.

1356

12 Oct 1915

DAILY AMMUNITION RETURN.

Piece	Projectile	Code	50	70	15	48	71	9	16	17	47	55	118	31 Bde	Total	Per piece
2.75	Guns															
	Shrapnel	P														
	H.E.	PX														
18-pr	Guns															
	Shrapnel	A	94	3				6	117	30				- 34	284	
	H.E.	AX	135	145				461	8	540				272 877	2138	
4.5" How.	Howitzers															
	Shrapnel	B												1 11	1	
	H.E.	BX													12	
6" How	Howitzers															
	Shrapnel	H														
	H.E.	F														
	A.P.															

B de Major

DAILY DIARY.

Z 2 group   13.10.15.

9th Batt.   Fired according to
            programme.

?th Batt.   Fired according to programme

118th Batt. Fired of enemy trenches SE
            of MINE POINT. Considerable
            damage was done to parapet.
            Fired according to programme.

47th Batt. Fired on AUCHY ALLEY
            Fired according to programme

General.
            12.15 pm and onwards
            enemy shelled our support and
            communication trenches, with
            light field guns + 4.2 How:
            There were no fires on German
            parapet.
            2 Red Lights went up in
            direction of MADAGASCA[R]
            about 2.20 pm.
                            L L Reeves 2/L
                            for Adj Z 2 group

"A" Form.   Army Form C. 2121.
MESSAGES AND SIGNALS.

TO	Ra 2nd DW

Sender's Number.	Day of Month.	In reply to Number	AAA
BG/184	13		

Daily Report 34th Brigade

50th Bty

6.20 am fired on trenches North of CANAL. 50 am retaliated on EMBANKMENT REDOUBT. 11am – 12.15 pm cut wire on South of Embankment. A lot of damage was done to stakes and wire. From 12 noon onwards carried out programme, also fired on houses in main road. Right Section fired occasionally on trenches S.W. of LES BRIQUES.

70th Bty.

Did not fire this morning. From 12 noon carried out programme. This is still being continued on AUCHY – HAISNES road.

(24)

7.30P

DAILY DIARY.
44th Bde
6-6 p.m. 12-13 Oct

Operations
  47th Div.
9.30 am Registered AUCHY ALLEY.
12-1 p.m. Fired at trench A28d1.5, A28d5.8
       — A28d6.6.
12.35-2 p.m. Fired at houses in A29c2.2
1.0-2.0 p. Fired at AUCHY.
2.0-2.30 p.m. Fired at trench A28d1.5 & A28d5.8.
2.30-6 p.m Fired at AUCHY ALLEY.

  56th Div.
9.55 am. Fired at RAILWAY EMBANKMENT in
     retaliation for shelling of HOLLOW.
12-1.0 p.m. Fired at trench A28d5.8 - A28d9.6.
1.0-6.0 p.m Fired at RAILWAY REDOUBT.

Information
       nil.

            [signature] Lt Col R.F.A.
                Comdg 44th Bde.

7.10 p.

			"A" Form.		Army Form C. 2121.
		MESSAGES AND SIGNALS.		No. of Message	

Prefix	Code.	m.	Words	Charge	This message is on a/c of :	Recd. at .... m.
Office of Origin and Service Instructions.			Sent			Date
			At .... m.		.... Service.	From
			To			By
			By		(Signature of "Franking Officer.")	

TO { ....

| Sender's Number. | Day of Month. | In reply to Number | **AAA** |

It was noticed by 50th Bty observer that the fires lit by the Enemy were not so effective as last time, and their rifle and machine gun fire much less in volume. Unaffected and healthy Germans were seen in EMBANKMENT REDOUBT, but none along the trenches. No patrols were sent out by our infantry.

Observation possible 6.30 - 7 am this morning. Light very good from 11 am onwards but country very much obscured by smoke after 1 pm.

Nothing further to report beyond what was sent in during afternoon. Our front all quiet.

Sheldard
Capt.

From
Place
Time

The above may be forwarded as now corrected. (Z)

Censor. Signature of Addressor or person authorised to telegraph in his name.

* This line should be erased if not required.

No. 22 Anti Aircraft Station

Return of Hostiles seen Engaged

Hostile Planes Seen		Position of Hostile Planes first Remarks		
Seen	Engaged	Battery	Action Taken	
			A.M.	P.M.
2.	1	ARLEQUIN	9.30	3.25

T. Newton
Capt. R.H.A.
Comdg 22 Anti Aircraft Section

15/10/15

No 98 Anti Aircraft Section
Shooting Report   C. Y. Ruse   os 19-15

Time	Objective	Rds fired	Remarks
3.25	German L.G.	1	

TCNewton
Capt. R.H.A.
Comdg 98 A.A. Section

13 Oct 15

DAILY AMMUNITION RETURN.

Picce	Projectile	Code	\multicolumn{9}{c	}{BATTERIES}	Total	Per piece
			50	70	15/48	71	9	16	17	47	55	B.Bde 178/31		
2.75	Guns													
	Shrapnel	P												
	H.E.	PX												
18-pr	Guns													
	Shrapnel	A	309	340	—	—	168	303	861	—	441	821	3243	
	H.E.	AX	128	260	—	—	344	27	544	—	492	1443	3058	
4.5" How.	Howitzers													
	Shrapnel	B												
	H.E.	BX					—	—	7	—	711	440	1151	
6" How	Howitzers													
	Shrapnel	H												
	H.E.	F												
	A.P.													

2nd Division Artillery Orders

by

Brigadier General G.H.SANDERS, D.S.O.,Cdg R.A., 2nd Divn.

13th October, 1915.

1040. R.A.ORDERS,

Were not issued on 12th Octr.1915.

1041. POSTINGS.

Major E.W.M.POWELL, D.S.O., from 48th Battery to command 41st Brigade; Vice Lt.Colonel RAVENHILL, C.M.G., to 26th Division, R.A., with effect from 5th October.

Captain H.F.GRANT SUTTIE to command 48th Battery; Vice Major E.W.M.POWELL, D.S.O., with effect from 14th October.

L.G.BUXTON. Capt, R.A.,

Staff Captain R.A., 2nd Divn.

- NOTICE -

A man capable of cooking for an Officers Mess is required at H.Q., 2nd Divn. Artillery.

Units having a suitable man desirous and recommended for this employment will submit names as soon as possible.

B Maj R 42nd D W G.539

At 8.15pm the 100th and 103rd Batteries stopped firing and 69th Battery opened on MAD ALLEY from MAD POINT to 74 and this barrage was kept up at slow rate till midnight when rate was quickened till 12.30am as the Queens reported that they would make a bombing attack at midnight. Slow rate was continued continued from 12.30 onwards. At 2.45am the Liaison officer with the Queens was called up and said the bombing attack had not taken place at midnight but was taking place at 2.45am. At 7.15am the OC 5th Bde asked for fire on the junction of LITTLE WILLIE and FOSSE trench. 2 guns of the 69th Bty are now firing up MAD ALLEY and 2 guns at the junction mentioned above

Rate of fire at MAD ALLEY 12 rds an hour.
   " " " " Junction 60 " " " "

At 7.25am I reported to GOC RA that we were not in LITTLE WILLIE and GOC 5th Inf Bde asked for fire on the trench from junction still new SAP northwards. We do not appear to be holding much North of Chord of cross the Redoubt.

H H Tondp
8.30am   Lt Col RM
14/10/15   Comdg 3rd Bde RHA

10:27 pm

B.Maj Ra 2nd Divn G 258.

Since 8 am there is little to report. Everything was very quiet in the Bde front and except for a certain number of whiz bangs no shelling of the Inf Bde trenches took place. The Batteries retaliated for these whiz bangs. Light very bad till noon when it improved and was excellent during the afternoon. There was very heavy bombing on HOHENZOLLERN redoubt between 1 and 3 pm. The GUILDFORD trench was plainly visible. It had reached within about 40 yds of the Redoubt. A little to the North of where it will eventually meet the redoubt German bombers were seen throwing bombs in a southerly direction. At about 2.30 pm a yellow flag was seen for the first time. A red & yellow screen was seen at the at 1. pm and the yellow flag was about 70 yards to the North of it. I am uncertain when the yellow and red screen was put up. It is in practically the same spot as yesterday afternoon. I saw it directly the mist lifted but it may have been left from yesterday. Our advance

2

seemed to make but little progress. Later on, from 3pm till dusk our guns both heavy & field fired at the German positions. There was not much retaliation.
The 69th Battery had one section on MAD ALLEY all day and 1 section on the junction between LITTLE WILLIE and FOSSE trench.
The 100th and 103rd did not fire except in retaliation till about 4pm when they fired on the front trenches in their zone.
At 6.30pm the 100th & 103rd ceased fire and the 69th will continue firing on MAD ALLEY, as last night.

7.15 pm

14/10/15.

Peter Bond Lt Col RFA
Cmdg 3rd Bde RFA

"A" Form.
Army Form C. 2121.

MESSAGES AND SIGNALS.

Prefix .... Code .... m.	Words	Charge	This message is on a/c of:	Recd. at .... m.
Office of Origin and Service Instructions.	Sent		.... Service.	Date ....
....	At .... m.			From ....
....	To			
....	By		(Signature of "Franking Officer.")	By ....

TO { Ra 2nd RW

| Sender's Number. | Day of Month. | In reply to Number | AAA |
| BG/186 | 14 | | |

Daily Report 34th Brigade
50th Bty
Fired a few H.E shell at trench about 100 yds S.E. of N.E brickstack where a new loophole was visible.
70th Bty
Fired on AUCHY-HAISNES road the whole 24 hours with 2 guns.
11.45 am retaliated on trenches.
This afternoon fired on TRIANGLE and main road when BRADDELL PT & HARLEY ST were shelled. Yesterday evening a gun was bulged. Report attached.
Observation possible 11.30 am today.
A little misty nearly all day.
Our front all quiet.

From
Place
Time

(16)

Oldfield
Capt.

The above may be forwarded as now corrected.   (Z)

Censor.   Signature of Addressor or person authorised to telegraph in his name.

* This line should be erased if not required.

DAILY DIARY.

Z 2 group.   14-10-15

9th Batt. during last night barraged Southern Exits of AUCHY. at 3pm today fired on houses in AUCHY and on movement observed on HAINES ridge.

118th Batt. fired on HAINES alley hill 8.55pm last night. Retaliated during night for bombs on R.S.F. 11 am fired on machine gun position 1pm " in retaliation for Phizz -bangs on Support trenches.

47th Batt nothing to report.

17th Batt. fired on RAILWAY HUT and manager's house in Fosse 8 group, otherwise nothing to report.

Continued increase of works on HAINES ridge. Germans shelled W. end of WILSONS WAY. railway arch S of 47th Batt (5.9) La Bassée road between Barricade and Harley ok (77 m)

(17) 8.3Pn   F. Rodd Lt.
                                Adj. 41st Bde.

DAILY DIARY.
44th Bde.
6-6 pm. 13-14 Oct.

Operations

56th Bty. 11.50 am fired at MINENWERFER in BRICKFIELDS at request of infantry.

Information.

10.15 – Hostile shelling on railway cneh about
10.45 am   F.10.C.1.1 with 5·9" from LA BASSEE direction.
4.10 pm   Also on CAMBRIN main road between BARRICADE & HARLEY STREET with 77 mm.

E.H. Harper Lt Col R.F.A.
Comdg 44th Bde.

112

No 44 Ack aerophotoplate

Bright laws gas? Engaged
Hostile Flash Allied Position of "Hostile Flash Post. Battery
seen   Battery   active Battery
                         A.M   P.M

Flash Engaged

ANTEQUIN

10

TO NEUVE   Capt. R.H.A.
              Bndy 82 R.A. Belin

14/10/15

119

22nd Aust. Aircraft Section
Shooting Report   to Y. Pr. 14-10-15

Line	Objective	Ras Lired	Remarks

T. Newton
Capt. R.H.A.
Comdg 22. A.A. Section

14/10/15

DAILY AMMUNITION RETURN.

14th Oct 15

Piece	Projectile	Code	50	70	15	48	71	9	16	17	47	55	118	81	&c	Total	Per piece
2.75	Guns																
	Shrapnel	P															
	H.E.	PX															
18-pr	Guns																
	Shrapnel	A	10	25	—	—	58	106	91	—	—	33	417			740	
	H.E.	AX	13	038	—	—	122	11	19	—	—	200	560			1163	
4.5" How.	Howitzers																
	Shrapnel	B															
	H.E.	BX						1	1	—	—	4				4	
6" How	Howitzers																
	Shrapnel	H															
	H.E.	F															
	A.P.																

2nd Division Artillery Orders

by

Brigadier-General G.H. SANDERS, D.S.O., Comg R.A., 2nd Divn.

14th October, 1915.

1042. RUM.

In future, the following will receive a daily full ration of rum when in the line :-

(i) R.A. personnel actually with Batteries.
(ii) Field Companies, R. Engrs.
(iii) Infantry Brigades.

Once a week a ration of rum will be issued to the whole division.

1043. STANDINGS FOR HORSES.

The black and red slack from the pits has proved fatal to horses in certain cases. Horses lick it and have died of acute irritation of the bowels.

This slack should not therefore be used except as a bottom to the standings, and should always be well covered with bricks or sand.

1044. LEAVE.

The daily allotment of leave for N.C.O's and men has been reduced to four per unit.

In accordance with the above the following will be the distribution until further orders :-

Friday.	41st Brigade.	4.
Saturday.	44th "	4.
Sunday.	D.A.C.	4.
Monday.	7th Mtn. Battery.	1.
	36th Brigade.	2.
	Spare.	1.
Tuesday.	34th Brigade.	1.
	41st "	2.
	44th "	1.
Wednesday.	34th "	4.
Thursday.	36th "	4.

L.G. BUXTON. Capt, R.A.,
Staff Captain, R.A., 2nd Divn.

Notice.

Yesterdays notice re cook for H.Q.R.A., is cancelled.

For Brigade Major.

DAILY DIARY.
44th Bde. RFA

Operations

56th Bty. RFA
4.35 p.m. Fired 8 rounds at Brickstack C. (A.21.b.9.9.) at request of infantry to stop MINENWERFER

Information

14.10.15   11.50 p.m. Enemy shelled houses in vicinity of ANNEQUIN CHURCH with 105 mm howitzer, and again at 2. a.m. 15.10.15.

15.10.15. All day intermittently enemy shelled our trenches opposite HOHENZOLLERN REDOUBT

M.V. Jackworth.
Lt. RFA
for Lt. Col. RFA
Cmdg. 44th Bde. RFA

DAILY DIARY.

Z group.   15-10-16.

9th Batt. fired on SOUTHERN
exits of AUCHY till 11 am. other
-wise nothing to report.

17th Batt. fired on LES BRIQUES
during the whole day. 1.20 pm
fired 12 rds on night lines
in retaliation to germans bombg
our trenches.

118th Batt fired on HAINES alley
during night. From 11 am till
8.45 pm onwards fired on
PEKIN alley and CEMETARY
alley. Fired on MINE Point
at request of infantry at 1.30 pm
to stop rifle grenades etc.

47th Batt till 11. am fired on
Southern portion of AUCHY

Too misty all day to observe.

F. Rodd. Mr
Adj. 41st Bde

			"A" Form.		Army Form C. 2121.
			MESSAGES AND SIGNALS.		No. of Message ....
Prefix	Code .... m.	Words	Charge	*This message is on a/c of:*	Recd. at .... m.
Office of Origin and Service Instructions.		Sent		.... Service.	Date ....
....		At .... m.			From ....
....		To			
....		By		(Signature of "Franking Officer.")	By ....

TO { Ra 2nd DW.

Sender's Number.	Day of Month.	In reply to Number	**AAA**
* BG/187	15		

Daily Report 34th Brigade

Too misty to observe except at short intervals. 50th Bty report that enemy have repaired most of damage done to wire & parapets. 70th Bty retaliated on brickstacks from where a trench mortar was firing (probably between 'D' & 'E' brickstack)

Our front all quiet.

Childard
Capt.

From
Place
Time

(10)

The above may be forwarded as now corrected. (Z)

Censor. Signature of Addresser or person authorised to telegraph in his name.

— B/Maj Ra 28rd Divn — G565

Progress Report.

All was quiet in the Bde front last night but heavy bombing was heard from the direction of the Redoubt. Glasgow Highlanders were digging a Sap along the AUCHY-VERMELLES road during the night. The 68th Battery fired intermittently throughout the night along MAD ALLEY. Our machine guns fired a good deal during the night. Otherwise there was no trouble.

Very misty all day and observation difficult. Fire was kept on all day by 69th Battery on MAD ALLEY and at 5.30pm the 100th Battery relieved the 69th at this task. 103rd are firing along the AUCHY-HAISNES Road.

Message received at 12.30pm that Germans were crumping trenches of Right Battn. The 146th Brigade were informed and they retaliated. Howr were also informed and information has since been received that we fired heavy shell at the German trenches in retaliation.

31 Bde H.Q. moved back from 5th Inf Bde Billets to ANNEQUIN at 6pm.

15/10/15

Brig. Maj R.A. 2nd Div.

HEADQUARTERS 31ST BRIGADE R.F.A.
Date 16/10/15
No. 61.935

I omitted in my report of yesterday evening, to state that an alternate line was laid by the B^de from Bn. H.Q. of the right Bn. of the 5th Inf. B^de at the QUARRY to gun's DRESSING STN. This line was laid by a different route as all wires have constantly been cut near the Railway lately. Commn. worked well during the night both with the QUARRY and the 146th F.A. B^de.

At 8.30 pm heavy bombing was heard by F.O.O's in the direction of the redoubt. The Oxfords extended GUILDFORD TRENCH towards the Redoubt but I have received no report that a junction has been effected. so I report He is in that work is still going on there. My F.O.O. went out at 12 midnight with O.C. Oxfords to take bearing of a light on the Redoubt. No light was apparently shown by 46th Div. The enemy shelled our support trenches during the night and also the QUARRY. & 149th Bty retaliated. At 8 am GUILDFORD TRENCH was shelled by heavy Howitzers and a Battery was turned on in retaliation by 146th B^de & the matter was reported to you with request for assistance from Heavy guns.

9 am 16/10/15.

JobBradford Lt Col R.A.
Comdg 31st B^de R.F.A.

72

No. 22 Anti Aircraft Section
Casualty Return
10.10.15

Officers — Nil Remarks

Other Ranks

M2/07756 Pte L.B. Taylor ASC MT
M/057102 " S.R. Arnold   "   "
to base

T.C. Newton
Sgt i/c
Coy HQ 22 AA Section

10.10.15

No. 22 Aut. Aircraft Section 115

Ready & Boothlands Gun & Engaged
Gutter Pillness Pillness of
          Gun   Battery   Gutts Plane Fired
                              Cotters released
                              A.M. P.M.

Guns engaged   —   —

        —   A.M.E.QUIN —

                    T C Nestor Sgt. R.A.A
                                22. A.A. Sectors

19/3/41

122

Op 28 Oct. Giusseppi Ratico
Shooting Report

to Y. Pte 15-10-15

Aim	Difficulties	Regard	Remarks
	points	rest	

T.C.Newton — Capt. R.A.M.
L.O. R.A. A. Section

15/10/15

SECRET. Copy No. 4

2ND DIVISION OPERATION ORDER No. 69.

Reference BETHUNE Combined Sheet and
Trench Map,36.c.NW,Sheet 1, 1/10,000.

15th October, 1915.

1. Tomorrow, the 16th instant, 19th Infantry Brigade will relieve 20th Infantry Brigade, 7th Division,(Headquarters CHEMISTS SHOP) in the line from R.1 inclusive to the LA BASSEE road exclusive, under arrangements to be made direct between Brigade Commanders concerned.

2. The Section includes ARTHUR'S KEEP and RUSSELL'S KEEP. The Northern boundary will be the main road exclusive as far West as CAMBRIN SUPPORT POINT, thence so as to include the whole of ANNEQUIN and BEUVRY, and exclude LE PREOL and LE QUESNOY. The Southern boundary will be a line between R and R.1, thence just East of HEADQUARTERS TRENCH - junction of LEWIS ALLEY and HEADQUARTERS TRENCH exclusive - thence North of LEWIS KEEP leaving LEWIS ALLEY to 5th Infantry Brigade.

3. Artillery support will be given by 41st Brigade, R.F.A. under O.C., 41st Brigade, R.F.A. Headquarters A.19.d.0.0.

4. Two sections 5th Field Company, R.E. will be placed at the disposal of 19th Infantry Brigade by C.R.E. who will arrange details of R.E. relief, direct with C.R.E., 7th Division.

5. No.6 Trench Mortar Battery will be placed at the disposal of and will be attached to 19th Infantry Brigade. 19th Infantry Brigade will arrange direct with 6th Infantry Brigade to take over the section No.6 Trench Mortar Battery now attached to 6th Infantry Brigade.

6. 2nd Division will take over the evacuation of the above line under arrangements to be made direct between A.D's M.S., 2nd and 7th Divisions.

7. G.O.C., 19th Infantry Brigade will assume command when the relief is completed, and will report completion of relief to 2nd Division Headquarters.

for Lieut-Colonel,
S.G.S.O., 2nd Division.

Issued at 7-30 p.m. to :-
```
Copy No.1..... 5th Infantry Brigade.
  ,,   2..... 6th Infantry Brigade.
  ,,   3..... 19th Infantry Brigade.
  ,,   4..... R.A., 2nd Division.
  ,,   5..... R.E., 2nd Division.
  ,,   6..... Divisional Mounted Troops.
  ,,   7..... No.1 Bty. M.M.G.Service.
  ,,   8..... Divisional Signal Company.
  ,,   9..... A.D.M.S.
  ,,  10..... A.P.M.
  ,,  11..... "Q".
  ,,  12..... O.C., 2nd Divl. Train.
  ,,  13..... 1st Corps.            )
  ,,  14..... Adv. 7th Division.    )
  ,,  15..... Guards Division.      )   For information.
  ,,  16..... O.C., 186th Company,R.E.)
  ,,  17..... O.C., 187th   ,,    ,, )
  ,,Nos.18-22.G.S. and record.
```

DAILY AMMUNITION RETURN. —15th Oct 1915—

Piece	Projectile	Code	50	70	15	48	71	9	16	17	47	53	118	Total	Per piece
2.75	Guns Shrapnel	P													
	H.E.	PX													
18-pr	Guns Shrapnel	A		15				64	89	67	-	234	84	574	
	H.E.	AX		90				37	-	-		115	18	342	
4.5" How.	Shrapnel	B													
	H.E.	BX								-		12		12	
6" How	Howitzers Shrapnel	H													
	H.E.	F													
	A.P.														

"A" Form. Army Form C. 2121.
MESSAGES AND SIGNALS.

TO	31	44
	41	
	34	

| Sender's Number | Day of Month | In reply to Number | AAA |
| BM 5101 | 15 | | |

		RA	HQRS	well
close	at	LE QUESNAY		at
4 PM	and	will	open at	18
RUE	SAMI	CHARON	BETHUNE
at	the	same	hour
34	Bde	will	Remain	
under	command	of 7TH DIV		

From: Second Div Arty

(Z) BM

2nd Division Artillery Orders

BY

Brigadier-General G.H.SANDERS, D.S.O., Comdg R.A., 2nd Divn.

15th October, 1915.

1045. EQUIPMENT.

All bursts or bulged guns must be reported by wire to this office at once.- Nature of fuze and ammunition, and damage done to gun and personnel should be added.
Proceedings of Court of Enquiry should be forwarded later.

1046. PROFICIENCY PAY.

The following alterations in rates of Service and Proficiency Pay will take effect from 1st July, 1915:-

No.	Rank	Name	
68286.	a/Sgt.	George J.	Re-classified as Class 1.
71787.	Br.	Forsdyke. B.	" " "
64251.	Dr.	Allen E.J.	" " "
57168.	Dr.	Chapman J.	" " "
70731.	Gr.	Hill J.W.	" " "
61633.	Dr.	Hamilton R.	" " "
59862.	Gr.	Lamb C.H.	" " "
54178.	Dr.	Ward J.L.	" " "
34506.	Dr.	Watts J.	
68985.	Dr.	Brown O.	Granted Cl.1 P.P.@6d per diem
72515.	Dr.	Brown A.H.	" " " "
22091.	Dr.	Manley J.	" " " "
57519.	Dr.	Shaw J.E.	" " " "
9474.	Gr.	Stanfield T.W.	" " " "
69185.	Dr.	Thompson J.W.	" " " "
28539.	Dr.	Adams. F.	Granted Cl:1 Service Pay @ 6d per diem.

1047. TELEPHONE LINES.

Where telephone lines are laid in communication trenches they should be placed from 8 to 14 inches from the bottom of the trench, and not about waist high as at present where they are apt to get dragged out of position by portio of mens' equipment.

1048. HIGH TENSION POWER LINES.

No telephone wires are to be attached to the poles of high tension wires. Wires must be safeguarded where they cross the line of higher tension lines. power Lines

L.G.BUXTON. Capt, R.A.,
Staff Captain, R.A., 2nd Divn

FOUND -
A centre bar of fuze indicator T and P No.80 on the bank of the Canal on night of 14th inst.
Apply R.A., 2nd Division.

S E C R E T.   Copy 8

7TH DIVISION OPERATION ORDER NO. 51.
by
Major-General H. E. Watts, C.B., C.M.G.,
Commanding 7th Division.

October 16th, 1915.

1.   The 7th Division, less Artillery, will be relieved by the 2nd and 28th Divisions, and will move into the BUSNES area on relief.

2.   The 21st Infantry Brigade has already been relieved by the 83rd Infantry Brigade.

The 20th Infantry Brigade will on the 16th be relieved by the 19th Infantry Brigade.

The 22nd Infantry Brigade on the 17th inst. by the 83rd Infantry Brigade.

Battalions of the latter Brigade will not march from their billets before 9-30.a.m. on this date.

Details of the relief will be settled between Brigadiers concerned.

3.   Troops will move into their new area in accordance with attached march table.

4.   The relief of Field Ambulances will be settled between A.D.M.S. 7th Division, and A.D.M.Ss 2nd and 28th Divisions, with the limitation that they only move via roads North of the BETHUNE - CHOQUES - BUSNETTES Road and are clear of the road junction E.4.a. by 11.a.m. each day.

5.   No. 62. Trench Mortar Battery with personnel will be handed over to the 83rd Infantry Brigade of the 28th Division.

6.   Supply refilling point on relief will be selected by

the/

the A.A.&.Q.M.G., and notified to 1st Corps.

Supply refilling point for the 7th Division Artillery QUAI, BETHUNE.

Divisional Ammunition Column ANNEZIN.

7. The G.O.C. 2nd Division will assume command of the front South of the CAMBRIN - LA BASSEE Road on completion of the relief.

8. The G.O.C. 28th Division will assume command North of the LA BASSEE Road at 4.p.m. on the 17th, at which hour 7th Division Headquarters will open at Chateau BUSNES.

F. Gathorne Hardy
Lieut-Colonel.
General Staff, 7th Division..

Issued at 6 a.m. to :-

A.D.C. (for G.O.C.)	Copy No. 1.
G.S.O. 1.	" 2.
G.S.O. 2. (Office copy)	" 3.
A.A.&.Q.M.G.	" 4.
7th Signal Company.	" 5.
7th Cyclist Company.	" 6.
Divisional Sqdn.	" 7.
2nd Divisional Artillery.	" 8.
7th Divisional Artillery.	" 9.
C. R. E.	" 10.
20th Infantry Brigade.	" 11.
21st Infantry Brigade.	" 12.
22nd Infantry Brigade.	" 13.
A.D.M.S.	" 14.
7th Divisonal Train.	" 15.
1st Corps.	" 16.
2nd Division.	" 17.
28th Division.	" 18.
Meerut Division.	" 19.
170th)	" 20.
173rd) Field Company.R.E.	" 21.
186th)	" 22.
83rd Infantry Brigade.	" 23.

Date.	Unit.	From.	To.	Hour of march	Route.
16th.	20th Infantry Brigade.	trenches.	BETHUNE.		on relief by 19th Inf. Brigade.
	54th Field Coy. R.E. 95/3	LE QUESNOY. GORRE	BERGUETTE "		All troops are to march to the new area via roads North of the BETHUNE – CHOQUES – BUSNETTES road. Those moving to the BUSNES area on the 17th and the 18th are to be clear of the road junction H.4.a. by 11.a.m. each day.
17th.	20th Infantry Brigade.	BETHUNE	BUSNES area.	to march at 8.a.m.	
	Northumberland Hussars.	LE QUESNOY.	Fme du BLANC HANGAR.		
	Divisional Cyclists.	BETHUNE.	LE CORNET BOURGOIS.		
	22nd Infantry Brigade.	trenches.	BETHUNE.		
	Highland Field Company.	CAMBRIN.	BERGUETTE.	to march at 7-30.a.m.	
18th.	22nd Infantry Brigade.	BETHUNE.	BUSNES area.		
	Divisional Train.	BETHUNE.	CHATEAU DU QUESNOY.	to march at 8-30.a.m.	

N.B. A map of the billeting area is being issued.

SECRET.   Copy No. 8

7TH DIVISION OPERATION ORDER NO. 52.
by
Major-General H. E. Watts, C.B., C.M.G.,
Commanding 7th Division.

October 16th, 1915.

1.   The new area of the 7th Division having been altered, the 21st Infantry Brigade Group will move tomorrow to the area HAM en ARTOIS - BOURECQ - ST HILAIRE.

2.   The GONNEHEM area is to be cleared by, and the new area is not to be entered before, 4.p.m.

3.   Routes available: All roads North of the CHOQUES - LILLERS Road.

                                                  Lieut-Colonel.
                                        General Staff, 7th Division.

Issued at 11. p.m. to :-

A.D.C. (for G.O.C.)	Copy No. 1.
G.S.O. 1.	" 2.
G.S.O. 2. (Office Copy)	" 3.
A.A.&.Q.M.G.	" 4.
7th Signal Company.	" 5.
7th Cyclist Company.	" 6.
Divisional Squadron. N.H.	" 7.
2nd Divisional Artillery.	" 8.
7th Divisional Artillery.	" 9.
C.R.E.	" 10.
20th Infantry Brigade.	" 11.
21st Infantry Brigade.	" 12.
22nd Infantry Brigade.	" 13.
A.D.M.S.	" 14.
7th Divisional Train.	" 15.
1st Corps.	" 16.
2nd Division.	" 17.
28th Division.	" 18.
Meerut Division.	" 19.

DAILY AMMUNITION RETURN.

16th Oct 1915

Piece	Projectile	Code	\multicolumn{12}{c	}{BATTERIES}	Total	Per piece
			50	70	15	48	71	9	16	17	47	56	18	113/84		
2.75	Guns Shrapnel	P														
	H.E.	PX														
18-pr	Guns Shrapnel	A						150	39	8			3	125	325	
	H.E.	AX	39					125	-	-				2747	508	
4.5" How.	Howitzers Shrapnel	B								31					31	
	H.E.	BX								6					6	
6" How	Howitzers	H														
	Shrapnel	F														
	H.E.															
	A.P.															

370

"A" Form.
MESSAGES AND SIGNALS.
Army Form C. 2121.

TO: Ra 2nd DW

Sender's Number: BG/188
Day of Month: 16
AAA

Daily Report 34th Brigade

50th Bty.
Did not fire

70th Bty.
Fired on main road A22b2.8 in retaliation for shelling of barrier and main road at 2.35 & 3.40 pm.

No enemy movement or work seen

Observation very difficult owing to mist all day.

Oldacd

DAILY DIARY

Z 2 group.   16-10-15

9th Batt fired during last night on Southern exits of Auchy.
For rest of time all quiet.
118th Batt fired effectively on german front line to stop trench mortars
47th Batt (How.) Nothing to report.
17th Batt. fired at german front trenches to stop trench mortars. They ceased at once.

General. Too misty to observe. Germans shelled near Annequin church at 9 am 1 round 1.30 p 6 rds 4.2". Two casualties 47th B. Shelled support trenches A 20 d 7.7 with 4.2" and A 27 C 1.1 with Ptizz Lang.

F. Rodd Lt.
Adj. 41st Bde.

DAILY DIARY
44th Bde. R.F.A.
6 - 6 p.m. 15th - 16th October.

Operations

56th Bty. 3.25 p.m. Stopped a working party at A 16 c 3.4½.

Information

9 a.m. } Hostile shelling of houses in
& 1 p.m. } vicinity of ANNEQUIN CHURCH with 105 mm. from LA BASSEE
2.40 p.m. } Also of Support trenches at A 20 d 7.7
to 3 p.m. } with 105 mm.

M.S. Sankworth
Lt. R.F.A.
for Lt. Col. RFA
Cmdg. 44th Bde. R.F.A.

Bde Maj RA 2nd Divn —

No 957
Progress Report

Light very bad all day and observation practically impossible.

Retaliation carried out at 11 am, 1.30 pm and 3.35 pm by 69th Battery at request of Infantry.

100th Battery continued to fire all day along MAD ALLEY and retaliated twice at request of Infantry.

103rd fired all day at HAISNES Road slow rate of fire.

I visited trenches to see how our trenches run on HOHENZOLLERN redoubt.

A good view of GUNDFORD Trench can be seen from M3 and the Sap which at present being worked at to connect up with the Guards trenches is plainly visible. The screen put up on our trench on HOHENZOLLERN can also be seen. A junction should be effected by it.

[signature]

16/10/15   Cmdg 73rd Bde RFA

How shell (probably 4.5") were reported falling short opposite R1 trench and one shell fell in the R1 trenches. I also heard a complaint about our shells in the air was the nose caps falling short lately

1/22 Coln Usage Section
Sunday 17th 12-10-15

Time	Objective	Do face	1pm 12-10-15" Sanction
		—	
	—		
		—	
—			

16/10/15   T.C. Newton Capt. Pd.R.
            Comdg OC in Section

No 22 Div Mining Section

Return of Explosives used Fortnight

Places	Allied	Section of	Hostile Places used Hostile Wire
	seen	Section of Battery	
N/6/15			P.4
		ANNEQUIN	—
—	—		—
—	—		—

16/9/15

T C Newton
Capt R.E.
O/C 22 Coy R.E. Section

"A" Form.
MESSAGES AND SIGNALS.

Army Form C. 2121.

Prefix	Code	m.	Words	Charge	This message is on a/c of:	Recd. at	m.
Office of Origin and Service Instructions.			Sent			Date	
Secret			At	m.	Service.	From	
			To				
			By		(Signature of "Franking Officer.")	By	

TO	31st Arty Bde	34th Arty Bde
	41st "	"
	44th "	"

Sender's Number	Day of Month	In reply to Number	
BM 818	16th		AAA

To day 16th instant 19th Infy Bde will relieve 20th Infy Bde in the lines from R1 to the La BASSEE road aaa tomorrow 22nd Infy Bde will be relieved by the 83rd Infy Bde 28th Div aaa Second Div will take over command up to La BASSEE road from today aaa 28 Div will assume command North of LA BASSEE road 4 pm tomorrow

(818)

From Second Div Arty
Place
Time

The above may be forwarded as now corrected. (Z)

Censor.   Signature of Addressor or person authorised to telegraph in his name.

Major

*This line should be erased if not required.

Bde Maj Ra 2nd Div — Progress Report

All quiet during the night. 100th and 103rd Batteries continued their barrage as usual. Attack by Guards Divn on HOHENZOLLERN Redoubt started about 5 am.
Barrage discontinued at 10.5 am.
Retaliation by 69th Bty on German front trenches at 9.10 am.
HOHENZOLLERN and QUARRY and support trenches were heavily shelled all day. 69th Battery and 145th retaliated and help of Heavy Arty was asked for.
At 12 noon constant reports of shelling of our trenches came in so I ordered 65th Bty to fire 50 rounds H.E. into the trenches opposite. OC Bty said this had good effect.
VERMELLES was shelled at intervals, one 5.9 shell detonating in a bomb store throwing a large number of bombs high into the air where they burst. Small arms ammn was blown in to the 65th Bty position in large quantities. It was undamaged.
Several reports of our shells bursting very close to our trenches near GUILDFORD trench & S.A.P. have been sent in in the last 24 hours. It is believed that the shell come from the Canal NNW. The infantry report this direction.

17/10/15 J.H. Bruce Lt Col R.A.
Cmmdt 31, (13th) Bde

DAILY DIARY.

Z 2 group.   17-10-15.

9th Batt. fired during night on Southern exits of Auchy otherwise did not fire.

17th Batt. did not fire.

118th Batt. Fired on front trench in retaliation to Phizz bang. re-registered POPES NOSE.

47th Batt did not fire.

Too misty to observe, nothing to report.

S.C. 420 is being observed!

Rodd Lt.
Adj! 41st Bde.

The A.I. Auto Co. of India

Return of Weighbridge taken of Engages

Engine Number	Boiler	Leading or Bogie	Leading Driver Wheel	Driver Wheels		
				Total between		
				F.R.	R.R.	
Engaged						
			AMBURN			
				—		

T. N...
Lall F.N.
Engr. RS A. P. Walker

17/9/15

129

No 22 A.E. Siege Bt Section

1st Hostile q Report   6 9 pm 14-10-15

Time	Objective	Replied	Remarks

T C Newton Capt R.H.A
Comdg 22. A.A Section

11/10/15

"A" Form.   Army Form C. 2121.
MESSAGES AND SIGNALS

TO: RA 1st Corps

Sender's Number	Day of Month	In rep'y to Number	
BM 820	17	RA/5	AAA

34th Brigade aaa	50th —	F18a 1.1
	70th —	F24 c 9.2
41st Bde —	9th —	A 20 c 5.2
	17th —	F 24 a 8.2
	118th —	F 24 c 8.9
31st Bde —	103rd —	A 24 a 0.6
	100th —	G 2 a 6.2
	69th —	G 8 a 0.4
44th Bde —	47th —	F 30 c 6.3
	56th —	A 20 a 5.1

From: Second Div Arty
Place:
Time: 1. 20 1

Positions to fire on ground from K5 to Canal
(Supplied air Mines 1st lot)

Position	Nature	Fires on	Tenable in winter	Remarks
F29a17	18 pr.	A3d - A10c	yes	Emplacements now pulled down
F22c86	18 pr.	do	yes	Now used for S. of canal.
A14b.33	1/18 pr.	A8d	yes	
A9a0.3	1/18 pr.	A3	yes	
A13b54	18 pr.	A10 - Triangle	yes	
F17a1.1	18 pr.	do	yes	Might be needed for S. of canal.
● F11d35	18 pr.	A4d 10.10 -	yes	
F10d9.4	18 pr.	A23d5.0 do	yes	never used - & ready. 6 Emplacements.
F5c3.5	4.5 how.	S27 centre - A15	yes	
● 11a9.8	4.5 how	do. centre	no	never used.
F4d4.2	18 pr.	S27 centre - A9 centre	?	
F12c63	18 pr.	do	no	
F4d39	18 pr.	S28a - A10c	yes	
F11a35	18 pr.	S27 - A9	no	never used.
● S19d3.0	2/18 pr.	A4 - A9	yes	could take 4.
● 18a58	18 pr.	A9	yes	could take 8.
F12a107	18 pr.		no	wire cutting A9
F12a95	18 pr.		no	" " "
A7c36	18 pr.		yes	" " "
F4b44	18 pr.		yes	has been Shelled.
X28a35	18 pr.	K5 st	yes	
X22d53	18 pr.	K5 st	yes	
X28b83	18 pr.	do	yes	has been Shelled
F15c1.3	18 pr.	F11b - d	yes	not made - never used
F20b88	18 pr.	do -	yes	bad. Alt. t above.
F9a2.3	18 pr.	F12 a & C	yes	Partly made. never used

F9C00	18/pr	F12aT C	yes	partly made, never used
F8632	4.5 how	F12	yes	" " "
F8A23	4.5 how	"	yes	never used.
F1693	18/pr	F12a	yes?	never used.
F2C22	18/pr	do	yes?	never used.

DAILY AMMUNITION RETURN.

17th Feb 1915

Piece	Projectile	Code	50	70	15	48	71	9	16	17	47	53	31/84	118	Total	Per piece
2.75	Guns															
	Shrapnel	P														
	H.E.	PX														
18-pr	Guns	30														
	Shrapnel	A	-	-	-	-	-	16	13	-	-	98			127	
	H.E.	AX	-	-	-	-	-	12	-	-	-	183	44		239	
4.5" How.	Howitzers	12														
	Shrapnel	B										13			13	
	H.E.	BX														
6" How	Howitzers															
	Shrapnel	H														
	H.E.	F														
	A.P.															

"A" Form.　　Army Form C. 2121.
MESSAGES AND SIGNALS.

| TO | 31 Bde |
| | 41 Bde |

Sender's Number: BM 822　　Day of Month: 17　　AAA

Resume barrage as last night and keep on till day is clear aaa acknowledge aaa

From: Second Div Arty
Time: 7.10 pm

BM RA 2 Dn

2nd Division Artillery Orders

by

Brigadier-General G.H.SANDERS, D.S.O., Comdg R.A., 2nd Divn.

17th October, 1915.

1049. HORSE RUGS.

The issue of horse rugs on a scale of one per horse for all units has been approved.
Indents for these will be submitted to D.A.D.O.S.

1050. STANDINGS FOR HORSES.

Reference R.R.Order No.1043, d/14-10-1915 - re slag for standings.
It has now been decided that this slag should not be covered with sand but with bricks only.

1051. DESPATCHES.

Despatches for units will leave Head Quarters at 9 a.m., 2 p.m., and 7 p.m. daily.

1052. TRAFFIC.

Bridge over canal at E.5.d.5.2., BETHUNE Sheet 1/40,000 is closed to all traffic for repair until further notice.

1053. HORSE LINES.

The Corps Commander wishes immediate steps to be taken to provide slag for horse lines of Divisional Cavalry and Regimental Transport. The slag which can be obtained from the FOSSE at ANNEZIN should be covered over by a layer of earth and well beaten down. The entrances to any orchards should also be slagged over.
To ensure continuity of work, and satisfactory results units on relief or otherwise, will take over and continue work on standings already commenced.

L.G.BUXTON. Capt, R.A.,

Staff Captain, R.A., 2nd Divn.

Bde Maj RA 2nd Divn.

18/10/15
6963

All quiet during the night. There were complaints from the Infantry (Right Bn of 5th Bde) that our shells were falling short near Guildford Trench. As there have been so many complaints I sent my forward officer down into this trench to investigate. At midnight he reported that he had visited the trench and whilst there 2 of our shells, at 11.35 pm and 11.40 pm, fell behind him when he was at C4 a 10.4. 15 south of the GUILDFORD trench and between it and our front line trenches.

A message came at 12.20 from Right Bn asking that fire of our guns could be raised saying that shells were hitting the parapet and destroying the wire of their right front trench.

A further report from Infantry states that a shell dropped in first T head of Guildford trench at 4.49 am. The case has been found and I am going to the trench to investigate this morning.

18/10/15

L W Bradfield
Cmdg 31st Bde R.F.A.

Later
Marks on this shell are N 44 B
according to Infy. (firmer)
8.20 am

DAILY DIARY
44th Bde. RFA
6-6 p.m. 17th-18th Oct.

Operations

47th Bty. 12.30 p.m. Registered
RYAN'S KEEP   A22 c 2.2
FRANK'S KEEP A22 a 0.2

56th Bty.
11.8 a.m. ⎫ Retaliated on trenches near
to 12.25 p.m ⎭ N.E. BRICKSTACK whence
heavy MINENWERFER active and
effective on HOLLOW was reported to
be firing. MINENWERFER eventually
stopped firing.
2.57 p.m. Registered work at A 10. d 8.5
(cooperation in event of attack on Indian
Corps.)

Information 4.30 p.m ⎫ Hostile shelling of
to 5 p.m ⎭ A 20 d 5.6.

W.S. Barkworth.
Lt. RFA
for O.C. 44th Bde
RFA.

DAILY DIARY

Z 2 group.   17-10-15

9ᵗʰ Batt fired in retaliation to Phizz bangs on trenches at 10am
Fired on working party 21 B 2.3 and again on german front trenches 4.30pm to 5pm

118ᵗʰ Fired on MINE Point to stop minenwerfer. 9.30 am

17ᵗʰ Batt Registered RYANS Keep and FRANK'S keep.

17ᵗʰ Batt fired twice on enemy front line by request of infantry to stop trench mortar fire.

General. Germans shelled 9th and 47th O.P. owing to infantry working parties appearing on Maison Rouge crest about 100x in front of O/Po digging a trench. Two direct hits on 47th one on 9th Batt O.P.

German front parapet has been strengthened and new wire placed in front of 9th Batt zone.

F. Roddel M
Adjt 41st B'de

DAILY DIARY
44th Bde R.F.A.
6–6 p.m. 16th – 17th October.

Operations

56th Bty.   6.20 p.m. ⎫ Fired at MINENWERFER
16.10.15   8.15 p.m. ⎬ in BRICKFIELDS at
            9.5 p.m. ⎭ request of infantry.
On latter occasion infantry
reported direct hit, and it
has not fired since then.

Information Too misty for observation.

17.10.15
                    M.W.Sackworth
                            Lt. R.F.A.
                    for O.C. 44th Bde. R.F.A.

No. 22 Anti Aircraft Section

Shooting Report 6 Ypres 18-10-15

Time	Objective	Observation	Remarks

18/10/15

T Newton
Capt. R.H.A
Comdg. 22. A.A Section

No. 22. A.A. Section

Return of Aeroplanes engaged   18.10.15

Hostile Planes engaged	Allied Aero	Position of Battery	Hostile Planes most active between		Remarks
			A.M.	P.M.	
	15	ANNEQUIN	—	—	1 Plane passed over at 8.25 A.M. travelling E to N. but could not be recognised owing to the mist

T C Newton Capt RFA
Comdg. A.A. Section

18/10/15

DAILY AMMUNITION RETURN. Expended 18/10/15

Piece	Projectile	Code	50	70	15	48	71	9	16	17	47	55	34	118			Total	Per piece
2.75	Guns																	
	Shrapnel	P																
	H.E.	PX																
18-pr	Guns																	
	Shrapnel	A	19					38	34		76						162	
	H.E.	AX		18				138		122	251						419	
4.5" How.	Howitzers																	
	Shrapnel	B									15						15	
	H.E.	BX								7 31	85						123	
6" How	Howitzers																	
	Shrapnel	H																
	H.E.	F																
	A.P.																	

1380

"A" Form.
MESSAGES AND SIGNALS.
Army Form C.
N. of Message

| Prefix | Code | m. | Words | Charge | | This message is on a/c of: | Recd. at | m. |

Office of Origin and Service Instructions.

Sent
At ..... m.
To .....
By .....
(Signature of "Franking Officer.")

Date .....
From .....
By .....

TO { 31"
       41"   ~~Bde~~ Brigades

| Sender's Number | Day of Month | In reply to Number | AAA |
| BM 527 | 18 | | |

Night firing aaa Ordinary
defensive arrangements
aaa

From   Second Div Arty
Place
Time   5.30 pm

The above may be forwarded as now corrected.
Censor.   (Z)   Signature of Addresser
                   BM R.A. 2 Div.
* This line should be erased if not required.

2nd Division Artillery Orders

by

Brigadier-General G.H.SANDERS, D.S.O., Comdg R.A., 2nd Divn.

18th October, 1915.

1054. OFFICERS' LEAVE.

Leave for officers will be given at the rate of one officer every other day per brigade, in the following order,- 34th, 36th, 41st, 44th briagdes and D.A.C. The 34th Brigade will send their first officer on Wednesday next, 20th October. Applications should reach this office two days previous to the date on which it is intended that the officer should leave.

L.G.BUXTON. Capt, R.A.,
Staff Captain, R.A., 2nd Divn.

"B" to Maj. R.A. 2nd Div:— 978

Since report this morning I saw the cases of shell reported to have fallen in our trenches at [struck] at 4.40 a.m. They were cases of 18 pr shrapnel. They were shewn to me at Battn Hd qrs at the Quarry. I visited the front trenches of the 1/4 K¹ Battalion of 5th Bde and saw where the parapets had been struck by our shell. There seemed great doubt [struck] amongst the 1/4 K⁴ as to the exact positions of the sap from GUILDFORD Trench and that from the Guards Division trenches on HOHENZOLLERN Redoubt. The Guards Sap was not visible at 1st from GUILDFORD Trench but on visiting the Guards Sap and looking through a periscope everything was quite clear. The end of the original GUILDFORD Trench was plainly visible. The Sap out of this trench to meet the GUARDS Sap was visible where my adjt raised a piece of paper on a stick. The ends of the saps were about 50 yds apart or less apart. It appeared to be [struck] but did not appear to be approaching one another. The rest of the German trench is about 50 yds from the Guards trench and there are barriers at each end. The Germans could be seen at their end from the end of the Guards Sap.

Some of our 18 pr shells were falling close to our trenches. It was impossible to tell the direction they came from but they did not appear very safe.

A few rounds were fired in retaliation at 9.45 am by 64th Bty.

Barrage on HAISNES Road was kept up by 103rd Bty till 6.30 am. 64th Bty on Mad ALLEY. Registration was also checked by 100th and 103rd Batteries.

Nothing more to report.

Geo Bradford Lt RA
Cmdg 3rd Bde RFA

18/10/15.

Observers of 64th Bty report nine knife rests have been placed in position at MAD POINT.

GB

DAILY DIARY
44th Bde R.F.A.
6–6 p.m. 18th – 19th Oct.

Operations   Nil

Information   Nil

19-10-15   W S Bankworth, RFA
                    for Lt Col RFA
                    Cmdg. 44th Bde.

B" Maj. R.A. 2nd Division.

All quiet during the night except for machine gun and rifle fire on working parties who were digging a trench between GUILDFORD and NEW trenches. Very little work I believe was possible. The sap connecting the Guards and GUILDFORD trenches was not completed according to the report of my F.O.O. at the Quarry. Nothing of importance during the day. Officers of each Battery visited the positions & Obs stns of the 9th Bde of the MEERUT Divl Arty with a view to taking over from them. At 5 p.m. a bombing attack supported by heavy field gun fire took place at HOHENZOLLERN redoubt. Our trenches were also shelled. The Batteries of this Bde retaliated on German trenches and ceased fire as soon as the forward Obs offrs reported all quiet. I simply ordered retaliation on trenches in our front as many other batteries were firing to the South towards the Redoubt. The attack / retaliation lasted for about ½ hour.

19/10/15

A. S. Douglas Cole R.A.
Cmmd 5th Bde R.F.A.

DAILY DIARY

Z a group.   19-10-16

9th Batt. fired on Trenches in retaliation to german fire on working party. 9th also shelled AUCHY A23 a 42. Shelled german trench during attack on HOHEN-ZOLLERN.

12th Batt fired on snipers post at 11.30am and 2.45 pm. Fired on front line at 5.15 in retaliation to german offenses.

118th Batt fired at 6am and 5pm to stop MINENWERFER. Just before 7pm barraged HAINES ALLEY.

47th Batt at 5.30pm fired on A29c 32 and 28d 9.6 in retaliation

17th Batt report Germans shelled BRADELL point with Phizzbangs where infantry continually show themselves.

9th Batt again report R.E. had fatigue parties about in the open on MAISON ROUGE ridge whereat the German shelled them. The German often shells this ridge now.

F. Rodd Lt.
Adj. 41st Bde.

No 22 Anti Aircraft Section

Shooting Report 5 to 4 pm 19.10.15

Time	Objective	Rds fired	Remarks
	—	—	—
	—	—	—
	—	—	—

19/10/15

T. C. Newton
Capt R.H.A.
Comdg. 22. A.A. Section

No 22 A.A. Section

Return of Aeroplanes Seen & Engaged. 19-10-15

Hostile Planes Allied Planes		Position of Battery	Hostile Planes Not Action taken		Remarks
Seen	Engaged		A.M.	P.M.	
1	1	MAREQUIN			
	10				

Newton Capt. R.A.R.
Comdg. 22 A.A. Section

19/10/15

SECRET.   Copy No. 4

                2nd DIVISION OPERATION ORDER NO. 70.

Reference Maps :-   19th October, 1915.
   BETHUNE Combined Sheet, 1/40,000.
   Trench Map, Sheet 36.c.NW.1, 1/10,000.

        1. 1st Corps is to hold the line from R.1 inclusive, N. of
    the VERMELLES - TRIANGLE Railway to THE LOOP A.3.c.3.7
    inclusive.

        2. On 21st October, 5th Infantry Brigade will be relieved by
    2nd Guards Brigade, Guards Division from G.4.a.7.4 to R.1
    exclusive.   Arrangements to be made direct between the
    Brigade Commanders concerned.
            Relief of the front line will start at 2 p.m.
            Route for 2nd Guards Brigade from South of Railway
    running from FOSSE 9.
            Route for 5th Infantry Brigade by RAILWAY ALLEY or LEWIS
    ALLEY and main LA BASSEE - BETHUNE Road.
            Dividing line between 2nd and Guards Divisions R.1 -
    HEADQUARTERS TRENCH - LEWIS ALLEY (all inclusive to 2nd
    Division) - along road in A.25.d. - Road junction F.30.a.4.0 -
    then to main road at F.29.b.0.7 - thence leaving main road
    inclusive to 2nd Division.

        3. On 21st October, 6th Infantry Brigade will relieve 19th
    Infantry Brigade from GUN STREET inclusive to the main
    LA BASSEE Road exclusive and will relieve 83rd Infantry
    Brigade, 28th Division from the main LA BASSEE Road inclusive
    to the CANAL inclusive.   Arrangements are to be made direct
    between Brigade Commanders concerned.
            Relief to be completed by 2 p.m.
            Route for 6th Infantry Brigade - BETHUNE and BEUVRY.
            Route for 83rd Infantry Brigade - ANNEQUIN and LE PREOL.
            6th Infantry Brigade will be responsible for PONT FIXE
    Defences and for finding the minimum garrison of the Keep of
    those Defences (one platoon).   The buildings within the
    defences of PONT FIXE on the N. side of the Canal will be at
    disposal of 28th Division for billeting purposes.
            Dividing line between 19th and 6th Infantry Brigades
    GUN STREET - THE LANE - Bridge at A.20.c.8.5 - centre of main
    road to Cross-roads F.30.a.2.8 - thence in a straight line to
    road junction F.29.a.   The LANE will be used by both Bdes.
            Dividing line between 2nd and 28th Divisions PONT FIXE
    (to 2nd Division) - straight line to bridge F.15.b. - along
    road to road junction F.14.b.6.9 - level crossing E.7.b.2.8 -
    then along the Canal.

        4. One brigade, R.F.A., 11th Corps will relieve 36th
    Brigade, R.F.A. at CUINCHY STATION.
            36th Brigade, R.F.A. will relieve part of 31st Brigade,
    R.F.A. 28th Division and will revert to 2nd Divisional
    Artillery.
            Reliefs to be completed by 8 p.m. 20th October.
            Details will be arranged direct between C.R.A's concerned.
            G.O.C., R.A., 2nd Division will be responsible for the
    artillery support of the front VERMELLES-AUCHY Road -
    VERMELLES-LA BASSEE Railway until 10 a.m., 20th October, when
    responsibility will pass to 11th Corps.
            Copies of programme of relief and movements consequent
    on above instructions are to be forwarded direct to 1st Corps.

                                                        5.

(2).

5. When the infantry reliefs are completed, the artillery defence of the 2nd Division front will be as under :-

Supporting 19th Inf.Bde... Under O.C., 41st Brigade, R.F.A.
                                      2 batteries, 41st F.A.Bde. *
                                      2 batteries, 36th F.A.Bde.
,,   6th ,, ,, ... Under O.C., 34th Brigade, R.F.A.
                                      2 batteries, 34th F.A.Bde.
,,   whole front.... Under O.C., 44th Brigade, R.F.A.
                                      44th F.A. (How.) Brigade.

* NOTE:- This group also covers part of 6th Inf.Bde.front.

6. C.R.E., 2nd Division will place 2 sections, 11th Fd.Co. R.E. at the disposal of 6th Infantry Brigade for work in CUINCHY Section. C.R.E. will arrange direct with C.R.E's of Guards and 28th Divisions for handing over and taking over R.E. duties in the present 5th Infantry Brigade and new 6th Infantry Brigade areas respectively.

7. The allotment of trench mortars will be detailed later.

8. Arrangements for billeting 5th Infantry Brigade on relief will be notified by D.A.A. & Q.M.G., 2nd Division.

9. A.D.M.S., 2nd Division will arrange direct with A.D's.M.S. Guards and 28th Divisions for the adjustment of the arrangements for the evacuation of the line given up or taken over by the 2nd Division consequent on these orders.

10. Command of the various sections will pass to the relieving Brigades and Divisions concerned on completion of each relief. Brigadiers, 2nd Division will report completion of relief of and by their brigades to 2nd Division Headquarters.

11. Report Centre unchanged.

                                                    Lieut-Colonel,
                                            S.G.S.O., 2nd Division.

Issued at 7.30 AM to :-
    Copy No.1..... 5th Infantry Brigade.
     ,,   2..... 6th Infantry Brigade.
     ,,   3..... 19th Infantry Brigade.
     ,,   4..... R.A., 2nd Division.
     ,,   5..... R.E., 2nd Division.
     ,,   6..... Divisional Mounted Troops.
     ,,   7..... No.1 Bty. M.M.G.Service.
     ,,   8..... Divisional Signal Company.
     ,,   9..... A.D.M.S.
     ,, 10..... A.P.M.
     ,, 11..... "Q".
     ,, 12..... O.C., 2nd Divisional Train.
     ,, 13..... 1st Corps.   )
     ,, 14..... Guards Division.)
     ,, 15..... 28th Division.   ) For information.
     ,, 16..... 170th Tunnelling Co.R.E)
     ,, 17..... 180th   ,,   ,,   )
     ,, Nos.
        18-22. G.S. and record.

Copy No. 11

S E C R E T.

2ND DIVISION ARTILLERY OPERATION ORDER No. 7.

19th October, 1915.

Reference Trench Map 36c N.W.1. 1/10,000.

1. 1st Corps is to hold the line from A 27b 8.0 (R.1.) to A 3c 3.7.(THE LOOP). 2nd Division is to hold the line South of the Canal.

2. On 21st October 5th Infantry Brigade will be relieved by XI Corps in front South of R.1.

(6)6th Infantry Brigade will relieve 19th Infantry Brigade on the front from A 21b 3.0 (GUN STREET) to the LABASSEE ROAD : and 83rd Infantry Brigade from LA BASSEE ROAD to CANAL.

3. 36th F.A.Brigade will be relieved by 62nd F.A.Brigade, 12th Division and will come under command of 2nd Division. Two batteries will go into action to relieve 31st F.A.Brigade, and will be placed under command of 41st F.A.Brigade. These reliefs will be completed by 8 p.m., 20th inst.

4. After reliefs 34th F.A.Brigade will be responsible for the front LA BASSEE Road to CANAL,(supporting 6th Infantry Brigade), and 41st F.A.Brigade for the front R.1. to LA BASSEE Road,(supporting 19th and part of 6th Infantry Brigades). Headquarters and one battery 36th F.A.Brigade will be in reserve. 44th F.A.Brigade will cover the whole front.

5. 41st Brigade will arrange to cover the front from R.1. to AUCHY VERMELLES Road up to 10 a.m., 21st inst, when when the responsibility will pass to the XIth Corps.

Major, R.A.,
Brigade Major, R.A. 2nd Div.

Issued at 11.15 a.m. to :-

Copy No. 1. to 34th F.A.Brigade.
2. " 36th "
3. " 41st "
4. " 44th "
5. " D.A.C.
6. " 2nd Divn. G.S.
7. " 1st Corps, R.A.
8. " 28th Division Artillery.
9. " 12th Division Artillery.
10. " 31st F.A.Brigade.

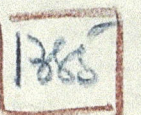

DAILY AMMUNITION RETURN. Expended 19th Oct. 1915

Piece	Projectile	Code	BATTERIES										Total	Per piece
			50	70	15	48	71	9	16	17	47	56		
2.75	Guns													
	Shrapnel	P												
	H.E.	PX												
18-pr	Guns													
	Shrapnel	A	43	6.				69	70	13	47	12	260	
	H.E.	AX	11	13				71	—	17	162	49	383	
4.5" How.	Howitzers													
	Shrapnel	B												
	H.E.	BX									14		14	
6" How	Howitzers	H												
	Shrapnel	F												
	H.E.													
	A.P.													

2nd Division Artillery Orders

by

Brigadier-General G.H.SANDERS, D.S.O., Comdg R.A., 2nd Divn.

19th October,1915.

1055. COURT MARTIAL.

A F.G.C.M., composed as under, will assemble at Headquarters, 44th B.A.C., Rue Gambetta, Bethune, at 10 a.m. on Thursday October 21st,1915, for the trial of No.57875, Gr. Gutteridge, 44th Brigade, and such other accused as may be brought before it :-

PRESIDENT.
Major W.F.JONES. 70th Battery, R.F.A.

MEMBERS.
Captain A.L.GRIFFITHS. 48th Battery, R.F.A.
Lieutenant T.F.V.HILLS.71st Battery. "

The accused will be warned and all witnesses required to attend.
The 44th Brigade will find a Court Orderly and necessary stationery.
Proceedings to be sent to Staff Captain, R.A. 2nd Divn

1056. TELEPHONE WIRES.

O.C. 2nd Division Signals in the course of the next few days will tap all telephone wires in 2nd Division area. If he fails to get a reply on any wire he will pick it up.

1057. ACCOMMODATION OF HORSES.

Houses, sheds, or barns which can be used as billets for troops are on no account to be used as stables for horses.

L.G.BUXTON. Capt, R.A.

Staff Captain, R.A., 2nd Divn.

DAILY DIARY

Z2 group.   20-10-16

9th Batt fired in repatriation on front trench, to trench mortars.
17th Batt fired 7 rounds on front trenches.

Remainder Nothing to Report.

15th Batt. relieved 69th Batt
71st Batt.   "   118th Batt

C and D/76 relieved two batteries
140th Bde and came under
41st Bde Control.
41st Bde. now control front from and including LITTLE WILLIE to La Bassée road.

J. Rodd Lt.
Adjt. 41st Bde

DAILY DIARY
44th Bde RFA
6-6 p.m. 19th - 20th October

Operations   Nil

Information   Nil

                    W. Duckworth
                         Lt RFA
                    for Lt Col. RFA
                    Cmdg. 44th Bde RFA

No. 22 Anti Aircraft Section

Shooting Report- 5 & 6 pm 20-10-15

Gun	Objective	Rds fired	Remarks
—	—	—	

20-10-15

J. Kent Lt. R.a.a
Cmr Capt. R.H.A.
Comdg 22 A.A. Section

No. 22 Anti Aircraft Section

Return of Aeroplanes seen & Engaged   20-10-15

Hostile Planes		Allied Seen	Destination of Battery	Hostile Planes that Battery believes		Remarks
Seen	Engaged			A.M.	P.M.	
1	1	1	Anne Quin		1	

20-10-15

E. Smith Lt. R.A.
for Capt R.H.A.
Comdg. 22 A.A. Section

[1389]

DAILY AMMUNITION RETURN. 20/10/15

Piece	Projectile	Code	BATTERIES							Total	Per piece
			50	70	15	48	71	9 16 17	47 53		
2.75	Guns										
	Shrapnel	P									
	H.E.	PX								36	11
18-pr	Guns										
	Shrapnel	A	2	-	7	-	-	11 8 8	- -		
	H.E.	AX	7	4							
4.5" How.	Howitzers										
	Shrapnel	B									
	H.E.	BX									
6" How	Howitzers										
	Shrapnel	H									
	H.E.	F									
	A.P.										

2nd Division Artillery Orders

by

Brigadier-General G.H.SANDERS, D.S.O., Comdg R.A., 2nd Divn.

20th October, 1915.

1058. PROMOTION - RECOMMENDATION FOR

O.C.Units will send in by evening of 23rd the names of any officers holding temporary commissions who are recommended for promotion.

1059. LEAVE.

Following is the new allotment of leave :-

Thursday.	21st Octr.	2 Officers.	7 men.	36th Brigade.
Friday.	22nd "	2 "	7 "	41st "
Saturday.	23rd "	1 "	8 "	44th "
Sunday.	24th "	1 "	8 "	D.A.C.
Monday.	25th "	2 "	-	34th Brigade.
			4 men.	36th "
			2 "	7th Mtn. Bty.
			1 man	Armoured Cars.
Tuesday.	26th Octr.	2 Officers.	-	26th Brigade.
			4 men	41st "
			2 "	34th "
			1 man.	44th "

L.G.BUXTON. Capt, R.A.

Staff Captain, R.A., 2nd Divn.

"A" Form.   Army Form C. 2121.

MESSAGES AND SIGNALS.

TO: RA 2nd DIV.

Sender's Number: BG/198   Day of Month: 21st   AAA

Daily Report 34th Brigade –

50th Bty.

Last night 10.30pm. retaliated on embankment at request of infantry who were being fired at with rifle grenades. Bty. has not fired today.

70th Bty.

Today – 4.5 pm & 4.50pm retaliated on trenches in reply to phizz bangs and trench mortars.

4.55pm fired on 'A' brickstack in reply to hostile 4.2" howitzer firing at our brickstacks.

Observation possible this morning 10.45 – 11 am. No enemy work observed. Our front all quiet.

Childard
Capt.

DAILY DIARY.

Z 2 group.   21-10-15

9th Batt. fired on working parties and movement seen in A 22 d 8·8, at 2.30pm.

15th Batt. all quiet fired registration rounds.

17th Batt. fired on German front trenches to stop bombing at 12.45 pm.

47th How Batt. registered with aeroplane. Registered FRANKS Keep RYANS Keep and comm. trench crossings behind MINE point.

71st Batt. Registered trenches front and second line and point A 29 C 5·3.

= Morning misty, light fair in afternoon. Working parties again walking about on MAISON ROUGE ridge.

<u>over.</u>

No fresh work observed. Germans shelled A20d 3.4 to 3.8 with 4.2" also W end of Vermelles.

Observation was impeded for 15th Batt by numerous officers of GUARDS DIV. coming to O.P.

F. Rodd Lt
Adj 41st Bde

DAILY DIARY
44th Bde R.F.A.
6–6 p.m. 20–21st Oct. 1915

Operations 56th Bty.

12 noon & onwards
Fired 8 rounds per hour on trench
A 28 d 4½.7½ – A 21 c 1.6 as per
programme.

3.15 p.m. Fired 7 rounds shrapnel at
working party in EMBANKMENT REDOUBT

5.40 p.m. Fired 6 rounds lyddite at
N.E. BRICKSTACK in retaliation for
shelling of our brickstacks.

Information Nil

21.10.15

M. W. Darkworth
Lt RFA
for Lt Col RFA
Cmdg 44th Bde RFA

No. 22 Anti Aircraft Section

Return of Aeroplanes Seen & Engaged 21-10-15

Hostile Planes		Allied Seen	Position of Battery	Hostile Planes most Active between		Remarks
Seen	Engaged			A.M.	P.M.	
x	—	17.	ANNEQUIN	—	4.10.	x Fighting British planes.

T C Newton Capt. R.H.A.
Comdg. 22 A.A. Station

21-10-15

No 22 Anti Aircraft Section

Shooting Report. to 4 pm 21-10-15

Time	Objective	Rds fired	Remarks
	—	—	

T Newton Capt R.H.A.
Comdg 22 Anti Aircraft Section

21-10-15

1392

DAILY AMMUNITION RETURN.

Exp^d. 21/10/15.

Piece	Projectile	Code	BATTERIES									Total	Per piece
			50	70	15	48	71	9	16	17	27	56		
2.75	Guns													
	Shrapnel	P												
	H.E.	PX												
18-pr	Guns													
	Shrapnel	A	6	2	59		108	7	45	-			225	
	H.E.	AX	-		30		-		27	-	3		60	
4.5" How.	Howitzers													
	Shrapnel	B									9			
	H.E.	BX									63	83	146	
6" How	Howitzers													
	Shrapnel	H												
	H.E.	F												
	A.P.													

2nd Division Artillery Orders

by

Brigadier-General G.H. SANDERS, D.S.O., Comdg R.A., 2nd Divn.

21st October, 1915.

1060. STANDINGS FOR HORSES.

Major General Commanding 2nd Division has given orders that standings for horses must be provided at once. It has been arranged that Motor lorries should carry the material from the mines, but units must continue to make standings with their own wagons. One of the brigades will be notified each evening of the number of lorries available for the next day's work, and a working party from that brigade will be at the mine dump selected at 8 a.m. to load the lorries. A N.C.O. should be sent to guide the lorries to the wagon lines, where another working party will be ready to unload. B.A.C's are included with the brigades.

L.G. BUXTON. Capt, R.A.,

Staff Captain, R.A., 2nd Division.

Daily Diary

56th Battery R.F.A.   21-22 Oct 1915

6 p.m. - 6 p.m. Fired on trench A28d 4½-7½ - A29c 1.6 at rate of 8 rounds per hour as per programme.

12.15 - 1 p.m. Fired at MINENWERFER about D Brickstack at request of infantry

3.40 - 4.10 p.m. Fired at working party in CANAL FORT

Information NIL

E.H. Harpur
Lieut-Col R.F.A.
Comd 44th Bde R.F.A.

22/10/15

GENERAL.

Germans shelled our front and support trenches today; also the barriers on road (4.2") and neighbourhood of 47th Batt.

Working party on ridge again in evidence, and got shelled.

Enemy have been working on craters A2, 1 & 6.4 some pit props and fresh earth was seen.

Observation good after 11. am

Rodolph
Adj. 41st Bde.

DAILY DIARY

Z2 group.   22-10-5.

9th Batt. fired on enemy's trenches in retaliation to Phizz Lang. Fired on wire laying party A22 b 5.4 and on working party A21 b 6.4 (see below)

15th Batt.

To Follow

17th Batt. fired twice today on SNIPERS post. fired at LES BRIQUES at 11.20am. fired on german trenches in retaliation.

47th How. Batt. fired on RYANS keep in retaliation to bombing. The following points were registered yesterday: RYANS KEEP: FRANKS KEEP: A22 c 6.0. A21 D 7.1. A22 d 1.0. A 28 a 15.35

71st Batt registered and verified points. Fired on RAILWAY trench in retaliation to German shelling

"C" Form (Duplicate). Army Form C.2123.

MESSAGES AND SIGNALS. No. Message

| | Charges to Pay. £ s. d. | Office Stamp. |

Service Instructions.

Handed in at .... Office ...... m. Received ...... m.

TO RA 2 Div

Sender's Number	Day of Month	In reply to Number	AAA
Addition to Daily Key aaa			
5th Batt registered and			
checked registration for			
MINNIE shoots			

FROM 41st Bde
PLACE & TIME 7.30 pm

(25555). M.R.Co., Ltd. Wt.W1789/1402. 70,000 Pads—6/15. Forms/C.2123.

"A" Form.   Army Form C. 2121.
MESSAGES AND SIGNALS.

TO: R.A. 2nd Divn.

Sender's Number: BG/203
Day of Month: 22nd
AAA

Daily Report 34th Bde.

"—" Battery. This morning at 12.15 pm and also at 1.15 pm fired on SINGLE TRUCK A.16.c.7.5½. which is suspected of being an observing Station, in retaliation for pip-squeaks on CUINCHY — a front trench. EMBANKMENT REDOUBT & TRIANGLE also engaged at these times.
At 3.20 pm & 4.30 pm fired on front & 2nd line trenches as enemy were shooting at our aeroplanes.

70th Bty. At 11.45 am retaliated on communication trenches for pip-squeaks down LA BASSÉE Road.
At 12.15 am fired on A.21.b.8.7. from whence a small trench mortar engaged our Brickstacks.

"A" Form.   Army Form C. 2121.

MESSAGES AND SIGNALS.

| TO | RA. 2nd Divn. |

| Sender's Number. | Day of Month. | In reply to Number | AAA |
| BG/203. | 22nd. | | |

Observation impossible from 4.30 pm. 21st
Till 8.30 - 9 am. 22nd.

Enemy fired on BRADDELL POINT and BARRIER where our infantry were working on trenches.

Good light. Wind S.S.W.

A Durand L.

22.10.15

Time: 6 pm.

1395

DAILY AMMUNITION RETURN. September 29/10/15

Piece	Projectile	Code	\multicolumn{9}{c	}{BATTERIES}	Total	Per piece
			50	70	15	48	71	9	16	17	47	56		
2.75	Guns													
	Shrapnel	P												
	H.E.	PX											285	
													81	
18-pr	Guns													
	Shrapnel	A	9	5	7	-	48	46	21	18				
	H.E.	AX	49	8	-	-	-	9	-	15				
4.5" How.	Howitzers													
	Shrapnel	B						-	20				20	
	H.E.	BX						-	216|			216	
6" How	Howitzers													
	Shrapnel	H												
	H.E.	F												
	A.P.													

"A" Form.   Army Form C. 2121.

MESSAGES AND SIGNALS.

Prefix... Code... m.	Words	Charge	This message is on a/c of:	Recd. at ... m.
Office of Origin and Service Instructions.	Sent			Date
	At ... m.		Service.	From
	To			
	By		(Signature of "Franking Officer.")	By

TO { (I)   RA. 2nd Divn.

| Sender's Number. | Day of Month. | In reply to Number | AAA |
| OK/8. | 23d. | | |

Daily Report 34th Bde.

50th Bty.

At 2.30 pm. retaliated for pip-squeaks on our trenches by shooting at House at A.16.d.8.3. suspected as being H.Q. at Battery position A.17.d.3.2. at Single Truck A.16.c.7.5 suspected as being observation post. & at 'embankment redoubt'.

At 3.30 pm. on TRIANGLE in retaliation for minenwerfer firing on HOLLOW & CANAL FORT. minenwerfer not located.

70th Bty.

At 11.30 am fired 2 Test rounds on A.1.b. At 11.40 am fired on trench mortar located at A.21.8.87. At 2.20 pm in retaliation for pip-squeaks firing on STAFFORD REDOUBT.

The above may be forwarded as now corrected.   (Z)

Censor.   Signature of Addressor or person authorised to telegraph in his name.

* This line should be erased if not required.

"A" Form.
MESSAGES AND SIGNALS.
Army Form C. 2121.

| TO | RA 2nd Divn. |

Sender's Number.	Day of Month.	In reply to Number	AAA
BK/8.	23rd	contd.	

Observation impossible between 5 p.m. on 22nd and 11.30 a.m. 23rd.

During night 22/23rd the row of large trees running from SPOTTED DOG P.H. to road at A.16.c.9.1. were cut down, about 20 trees in all, opening up a view of houses in A.16.d & A.17.c. from BRADDELL POINT.

Light poor all day. Slight Wind S.W.

23.10.15.

A Durand Lt.
Adj 34th Bde.

DAILY DIARY

Z.2 group   23-10-16

9½ Batt. fired on crater a21b6 3½ where enemy have done work. Fired at suspected O.P. about A23a 1.0. four hits low down were scored.

15ᵗʰ Batt. fired on trench near POPES NOSE this morning. also shelled vicinity of MINE Point with 30 rounds during the middle part of day.

17ᵗʰ Batt. at 3 pm fired 45 rounds at German trenches. At 3.50 pm fired on W. exits of Auchy. The enemy shelled our trenches about this time.

71ˢᵗ Batt. fired on MINE point AUCHY and Auchy alley.

47ᵗʰ How Batt. fired on RYANS KEEP at request of infantry 12·45 pm 4 rds.

In addition to above 15ᵗʰ & 71ˢᵗ Batt shot at german wiring parties below ~~our~~ Mine point at 11 pm last night. The Infantry reported this shoot quite successful an officers patrol having previously reported the ~~patrol~~ parties hard at work. The 4.7" How batt fired on RYANS KEEP and A21d 7·1 at 11.15 11.20 and 11.25 pm

The above treatment will be repeated tonight at 9 pm.

Germans retaliated a certain amount this afternoon on our trenches as a result of our fire.

The work in the craters (reported under 9th Batt) seems to be a fairly large undertaking. 18 pr traj. is however too flat to get well into the place a 4.5" How would be better. The germans retaliated to 9th Batt fire with Trench mortars.

Germans shelled VERMELLES cross roads with 15 cm.

Light very bad all day.

23-10-15.

F Rodd Lt
Adj. 4½ Bde

DAILY DIARY
44th Bde RFA
6-6 p.m. 22-23 Oct. 1915

Operations 56th Bty.

6 p.m - 6 p.m. Bombardment of trench A 28 d 4½.7½ — A 29 c 1.6 at 8 rounds per hour as per programme

11.20 p.m. Fired 7 rounds in reply to trench mortar at request of 5th Kings

1.35 p.m. Fired on BRICKSTACKS C & D in reply to trench mortars.

3.35 p.m. Fired on EMBANKMENT REDOUBT & TORTOISE in retaliation to enemy shelling with heavy howitzers & minenwerfer.

23-10-15

W.W. Barkworth
H.O.W.A.
for Lt. Col. RFA
Cmdg 44th Bde

R.A. 2nd Divn

About 12.45 p.m. today a premature occurred at the 56th Bty. when firing lyddite with No 100 fuze. One man was slightly wounded in the hand. Otherwise no damage was done. No explanation can be found.

W.S. Sankworth
Lt. R.F.A.
for Lt Col R.F.A.
Andg 44 D.B. Bde R.A.

No 23. Anti-Aircraft Section   14

Return of Aeroplanes seen engaged. 22.10.15

Hostile planes seen	Hostile planes seen engaged	Position of Battery	Hostile planes not action taken		Remarks
			A.M.	P.M.	
Engaged	19	ANNEQUIN	-	-	
Seen	-				

22/10/15

J.R. Murch Lieut R.A.
Comdg. 23. A.A. Section

No. 22. Anti-Aircraft Section.

Shooting Report to 7/pm 22.10.15"

Time	Objective	Rds fired	Remarks
		—	
		—	

J. Kraf Lieut R.F.A.
Comdg. 22. A.A. Section

22/10/15

DAILY AMMUNITION RETURN.

Piece	Projectile	Code	50	70	15	48	71	9	16	17	47	53	Total	Per piece
2.75	Guns													
	Shrapnel	P												
	H.E.	PX												
18-pr	Guns													
	Shrapnel	A	7	2	44	-	118	48	29	33	-	-	281	
	H.E.	AX	10	16	5	-	15	28	-	42	-	-	116	
4.5" How.	Howitzers													
	Shrapnel	B												
	H.E.	BX									1		210	
6" How	Howitzers													
	Shrapnel	H												
	H.E.	F												
	A.P.													

1397

2nd Division Artillery Orders

by

Brigadier-General G.H.SANDERS, D.S.O.,Comdg R.A.2ndDivn.

23rd October,1915.

1061. R.A.ORDERS.

Were not issued yesterday, 22-10-1915.

1062. DIVINE SERVICE.

All units R.F.A.,in or near BETHUNE will attend divine service in New Chapel, opposite prison,at 9-30 a.m to-morrow.

L.G.BUXTON. Capt, R.A.,
Staff Captain, R.A., 2nd Div.

DAILY DIARY

2" group.   24-10-15.

9th Batt. fired on working party A22a22 which was dispersed. From 3pm onwards fired on German trenches and suspected observing stations in retaliation to bombardment.

15th Batt. last night at 9pm fired on German wiring parties near POPES Nose. The Germans retaliated with MINNIE's whereat 15th Batt fired again. Also retaliated to German bombardment this afternoon, on support trenches etc.

17th Batt. fired on working party at A29a2.1.

71st Batt. fired on Houses in Auchy Les Brignes etc and shelled german support trenches in retaliation this afternoon. This battery fired in combined shoot last night at 9pm.

47th Batt (How). fired at 9pm 23rd on RYANS keep. with 71st and 15th. 47th Batt last night got on to hostile MINNIE in 50 secs and silenced it.

Germans shelled our trenches quite heavily with 77mm and heavy artillery our batteries retaliated firing about 150-200 rounds.

Germans also shelled VERMELLES intermittently with 10cm.

Observation possible 9 am but light very bad all day.

No fresh work seen

Rodd ?
Adj. 41? Bde

1399

"A" Form.
Army Form C. 2121.

MESSAGES AND SIGNALS.

TO: R.A. 2nd Divn.

Sender's Number: OK/13.
Day of Month: 24th
AAA

Daily Report

34th Bde.

50th Bty.

At 3.30 pm. fired on trenches in retaliation for pip-squeaks on the HOLLOW & communication trenches.

70th Bty.

At 10.10 am fired 2 Test rounds.
12.20 pm on working party seen at A.21.b.9.7.
3.5 - 3.55 - 4.15 pm in retaliation for trench mortar.

Observation impossible between 4.30 pm on 23rd and 10 am on 24th. Poor light all day.

Place/Time: 24.10.15.

A Durand
Adjt. 34th Bde.

DAILY DIARY
44th Bde.
6–6 p.m. 23–24 Oct. 1915.

Operations

56th Bty.

11.15 – 11.30 p.m. Fired at BRICKSTACKS in retaliation to MINENWERFER.

1.20 – 2.0 p.m. Fired at working party in PLAIN ALLEY with shrapnel

2.55 p.m. Fired at H brickstack as ordered.

6 – 6 p.m. Continued bombardment as per programme.

Information   Nil

24.10.15.

W S Bankworth
Lt & A
for Lt. Col.
Cmdg. 44th Bde.

DAILY AMMUNITION RETURN. Expended 24/10/15

Piece	Projectile	Code	50	70	15	48	71	9	16	17	47	53	Total	Per piece
2.75"	Guns													
	Shrapnel	P												
	H.E.	PX												
18-pr	Guns													
	Shrapnel	A	-	18	64	-	134	31	12	6	-	-	265	
	H.E.	AX	26	9	36	-	3	17	-	-	-	-	111	
4.5" How.	Howitzers													
	Shrapnel	B									-	17	17	
	H.E.	BX									9	213	222	
6" How	Howitzers													
	Shrapnel	H												
	H.E.	F												
	A.P.													

1400

2nd Division Artillery Orders

by

Brigadier-General G.H.SANDERS, D.S.O., Comdg R.A., 2nd Divn.

24th October, 1915.

1063. RIFLES.

The General Officer Commanding 1st Army does not propose to increase the present establishment of rifles in R.A. units.

L.G.BUXTON. Capt, R.A.,
Staff Captain, R.A., 2nd Divn.

Daily Diary
56th Battery R.F.A.
24-25th Oct 1915

Operations

9.5 p.m. in retaliation to MINENWERFER at request of Infantry

9.30 - 10.20 a.m. Fired in retaliation to 6" shelling Battalion H.Q. A 2 section

3.10 - 3.25 p.m. Fired on H. BRICKSTACK at request of 6th Inf: Bde

6 p.m - 6 p.m. Continued bombardment of Trench as per programme

Information : NIL

E.H. Harpur
Lt Col R.F.A.
Comdg 44th Bde R.F.A.

25/10/15

DAILY DIARY

Z group.   25-10-15

9th Batt. at 7.30 pm yesterday fired on Minenwerfer 21 B 8.3. and at 9.45 pm retaliated to Phizbangs. Today registered points in AUCHY.

15th Batt. fired on Minenwerfer at 9.30pm last night. Today fired on Les BRIQUES and POPES NOSE.

17th Batt. nothing to Report.

47th Batt. (Hows) fired on RYANS keep to stop Minenwerfer at 9.8 and 9.18 pm last night 4 rds each. otherwise all quiet.

71st Batt. fired on RAILWAY Tr. at 4.10pm today in retaliation

Light very bad all day. Germans shelled VERMELLES this evening (10 cm.)
Germans shelled our trenches yesterday evening and this evening
Infan to report a finger was blown into our trenches after explosion of one of our shell.

F. Rodd Lt.
Adj. 41st Bde.

"A" Form.
MESSAGES AND SIGNALS.
Army Form C. 2121.

| TO | R.A 2nd Divn |

Sender's Number.	Day of Month.	In reply to Number	AAA
OK/18	25th		

Daily Report 34th Bde.

50th Bty. Minenwerfers active at 9 pm. last night. (Howitzers replied.) No flashes observed.
At 9 am. enemy shelled A₂ with 4·2 How. — 50th Bty. retaliated on trenches; enemy did not cease till 4·5 How⁵ retaliated.
At 3.45 pm. fired in retaliation to pip-squeaks on A₂.

70th Bty. At 9.45 pm last night fired several bursts in retaliation for pip-squeaks from direction of AUCHY. At 10.15 & 10.45 am fired on working party carrying timber at A.22.a.8.9.

Observation impossible from 4.30 pm – 7.45 am. Light poor all day.

A Durand
Adj. 34th Bde.

Expended 25/10/15 — 1403

DAILY AMMUNITION RETURN

Piece	Projectile	Code	50	70	15	48	71	9	16	17	47	56	Total	Per piece
2.75	Guns Shrapnel	P												
	H.E.	PX												
18-pr	Guns Shrapnel	A	6	20	19	–	16	39	18	12			129	27
	H.E.	AX	14	11	2	–	–	–	1	–				
4.5" How.	Howitzers Shrapnel	B												
	H.E.	BX								8	235		243	
6" How	Howitzers Shrapnel	H												
	H.E.	F												
	A.P.													

2nd Division Artillery Orders

by

Brigadier-General G.H.SANDERS, D.S.O., Comdg R.A. 2nd Divn.

25th October, 1915.

1064. OFFICER'S POSTING.

Lieutenant A.A.M.DURAND is appointed acting adjutant 34th Brigade; vice Captain C. GELDARD appointed Brigade Major, R.A., with effect from 25th October.

1065. LEAVE.

Leave allotment for the ensuing week:-

Day	Date	Officers.	O.R.	Brigade.
Wednesday.	27th Octr.	2.		41st.
			7.	34th.
Thursday.	28th Octr.	2.		44th.
			7.	36th.
Friday.	29th Octr.	1.		D.A.C.
			8.	41st.
Saturday.	30th Octr.	2.		34th.
			7.	44th.
Sunday.	31st Octr.	2.		36th.
			7.	D.A.C.
Monday.	1st Novr.	1.		41st.
		1.		44th.
			4.	36th.
			2.	7th Mtn.
			1.	Spare.
Tuesday.	2nd Novr.	1.		41st.
		1.		44th.
			3.	41st.
			2.	34th
			1.	44th.
			1.	D.A.C.

1066. BILLETS,

All barns which have been put into a state of repair, and used as billets, are to be cleaned and whitewashed inside forthwith.

Requisitioning Officers will obtain the necessary whitewash and brushes by local purchase.

PTO

1067. AMMUNITION RETURNS.

Tomorrow's ammunition return will shew expenditure from 8 p.m. to-night until noon tomorrow.   In future returns will be from 12 noon to 12 noon.

L.G.BUXTON, Capt, R.A.,
Staff Captain, R.A., 2nd Divn.

Copy No. 4

2ND DIVISION OPERATION ORDER No. 71.
****

Reference Maps - BETHUNE Combined Sheet, 1/40,000,   25th October, 1915.
& Trench Map, Sheet 36.c.NW.1, 1/10,000.

1. 5th Infantry Brigade will relieve 19th Infantry Brigade in Section "Z" on October 29th, under arrangements to be made direct between Brigade Commanders concerned.

2. On relief, 19th Infantry Brigade will billet under arrangements which will be notified by D.A.A. & Q.M.G., 2nd Division.

3. 5th Field Company, R.E. will remain in their present area, and will be affiliated for work to 5th Infantry Brigade.

4. No.15 Trench Mortar Battery will remain attached to 5th Infantry Brigade for duty in the trenches. No.6 Trench Mortar Battery will remain in the trenches and will be attached to 5th Infantry Brigade.

5. G.O.C., 5th Infantry Brigade will assume command of "Z" Section when relief is completed, and will report completion of relief to 2nd Division.

Louis Vaughan

Lieut-Colonel,
S.G.S.O., 2nd Division.

Issued at 5.30 p.m. to :-
```
Copy.No.1.... 5th Infantry Brigade.
  ,,    2.... 6th Infantry Brigade.
  ,,    3.... 19th Infantry Brigade.
  ,,    4.... R.A., 2nd Division.
  ,,    5.... R.E., 2nd Division.
  ,,    6.... Divisional Mounted Troops.
  ,,    7.... No.1 Bty. M.M.G.Service.
  ,,    8.... Divisional Signal Company.
  ,,    9.... A.D.M.S.
  ,,   10.... A.P.M.
  ,,   11.... "Q".
  ,,   12.... 2nd Divisional Train.
  ,,   13.... 1st Corps.         )
  ,,   14.... 7th Division.      )
  ,,   15.... 12th Division.     ) For information.
  ,,   16.... 180th Tunnelling   )
                       Co.R.E.   )
  ,,   17.... 251st    ,,   ,,   )
  ,,   18.... 176th Spec.Co.R.E.)
  ,,19-23... G.S. and record.
```

"A" Form.   Army Form C. 2121.
MESSAGES AND SIGNALS.   No. of Message

Prefix	Code	m.	Words	Charge	This message is on a/c of:	Recd. at	m.
Office of Origin and Service Instructions.			Sent			Date	
			At	m.	...........Service.	From	
			To				
			By		(Signature of "Franking Officer.")	By	

| TO | { | R.A. 2nd Divn. |

Sender's Number.	Day of Month.	In reply to Number	AAA
OK/26.	26th		

Daily Report 34th Bde.

50th Bty.   At 3.15 pm. fired at trenches & Canal Bend.
At 4.30 pm along LA BASSEE road.

70th Bty.   At 12.10 & 3.45 pm. fired on trenches both first line & communication in retaliation for pip.squeaks on PARK LANE REDOUBT.

① Observation impossible between 4.30 pm & 6 a.m. Very good light all day.

② In A2 the enemy put up a large cross between the lines. The following is printed on it in black — "FOR KING & FATHERLAND. DIED AS HEROES — LT. KING LT. HALL & 8 men of S. STAFFS. BURIED by 6/SPARR.

From ③
Place: Neighbourhood of "KINGSCLERE"   A. Durand
Time: Shelled with 8" at 12.40 p.m.   Adj. 34th Bde.

DAILY DIARY.

Z. group.   26-10-15

9th Batt fired on house where party was observed putting up a green screen A 22 d 8 7. Registered and fired on suspected billet A 18 d 8 8. Considerable movement was seen between houses A 19 a 0·5. This was shelled intermittently whenever Germans were seen. Gun position A 22 d 2·9 was registered and two rounds put into the aperture.

15th Batt. fired on junction of Auchy and Pekin alley also on Lone farm. A new trench A 28 b 2·1 registered (see below)

17th Batt. registered Dove alley east, and following points from Fosse 9 Siding B 19 c 1·7. Auchy cemetary. Railway W. of LES BRIQUES. Also fired on HAINES + roads.

47th How. Batt. registered new trench A 28 b 2·1 (see below). "Special" shell were used this afternoon.

71st Batt fired on AUCHY. WATER tower Auchy. RAILWAY tr and house A 30 a 6·2

ENEMY SHELLING. Hostile shelling rather more active today. Road junction F29A48 was shelled this morning 8 am. A very fine deep crater was made in the middle of pavé. Also some 105m hostile shell fell in A29c. Our trenches were shelled (77mm) at about 8 am. 11.15am 1.40pm etc. 105 cm shell fell G7B.

RETALIATION. Germans required retaliating on their trenches by 9th 17th etc intermittently 4 or 5 times.

FRESH WORK a new trench was observed by 15th and 47th as per sketch. The wire is on _inside_ of triangle. It appears to be for the purpose of establishing a defensive flank facing south or north; as well as for a possible evacuation of MAD Point as a result of a withdrawal from Fosse 8.

The wire along trench from LONE Farm to CORONS is on EAST side.

Nearly all the comm. trenches in the vicinity of LONE farm and N of CORONS have been prepared for fire trenches.
The wire round PEKIN trench

is very strong and very broad.

Light very good today: first day it has been possible to prepare ARCS of VISION from O.Bo

Report on 4.5" "Special" shell to follow.

Todd
Adj. 41st Bde.

FD1/4

R.A. II Div.

Reference air photograph 1462 of 22-9-15 could not keep shew at crossing where DOCK ALLEY crosses railway at 22c 7.5-6 be given a name. I understand the work on railway at 28a 1.2- is now known as RAILWAY WORK

25-10-15

T. Rodd
Adj. 41½ Bde

Daily Diary
56th Battery 25th–26th Oct 1915

__Operations__

6 p.m. – 12 noon Fired at trench according to programme

9.10 – 9.50 a.m. Fired at H Brickstack at request of 6th Inf Bde; 8 direct hits

2.55 – 3.30 p.m. Fired Shrapnel at working party in PLAIN ALLEY

__Information__

NIL

C.H. Harpur
Lt Col R.F.A.
Comdg 44th Bde R.F.A.

26/10/15

"A" Form.
MESSAGES AND SIGNALS.
Army Form C. 2121.

TO	RA 2nd Div.

Sender's Number.	Day of Month	In reply to Number	AAA
B/46	26th		

Tactical return aaa Battalion Head Qrs. A.2 shelled with 105mm now. at 1.30pm aaa A white cross has appeared at A.16.C.1.7½ bearing the inscription "For King and the Fatherland died as heroes LT KING LT HALL and 8 men of the South Staffordshire regt. buried by 6/5 parr

From: 44th Bde
Place:
Time: 3.45pm

26th Oct 1915

DAILY AMMUNITION RETURN.

Piece	Projectile	Code	50	70	15	48	71	9	16	17	47	58	Total	Per piece
2.75	Guns Shrapnel	P												
	H.E.	PX												
18-pr	Guns Shrapnel	A	-	-	-	56	47	2	42	-	-		147	
	H.E.	AX	-	-	-	25	35	-	9	-	-		69	
4.5" How.	Howitzers Shrapnel	B												
	H.E.	BX					-		137				137	
6" How	Howitzers Shrapnel	H												
	H.E.	F												
	A.P.													

1407

2nd Division Artillery Orders

by

Brigadier-General G.H.SANDERS, D.S.O., Comdg.R.A., 2nd Divn.

26th October, 1915.

1068. CASUALTY RETURNS.

Until further orders the Daily Casualty Return will be rendered at the same time and for the same period as the daily ammunition returns.

L.G.BUXTON, Capt, R.A.,
Staff Captain, R.A., 2nd Divn.

Daily Diary

56th Batt.y 26-27th Oct 1915

Operations 7.15–7.52 p.m. Fired at MINENWERFER at request of Infantry

12.5–1.10 p.m. Retaliated to MINENWERFER and shelling of HOLLOW by 4.2" at request of Infantry

2.30–4.5 p.m. Registered following Points
Support Trench A9d 8.8 – A9b 6.1
Front Trench A9d 8.2 – 8.5
Communication Trench & bend westwards
Northwards A10c ½.4 – 3½.5 – 3.7½

Aeroplane went up about 3.30 p.m. to register Trench A28d 4½.7½ – A.29c 1.6 without giving any warning but descended owing to Engine trouble.

E.H. Harpur
Lieut-Col R.F.A.
Comdg 44th Bde R.F.A.

27/10/15

"A" Form.   Army Form C. 2121.

MESSAGES AND SIGNALS.

TO	R.A 2nd Div.		
Sender's Number. OK/31	**Day of Month.** 27th	**In reply to Number**	**AAA**
	Daily Report 34th Bde		
50th Bty.	7.30 p.m (26th) fired at request of infantry in reply to trench mortars. 9.20 a.m. (27th) fired at support trenches from which thick volumes of smoke were issueing. At 12.15 pm & 1 pm registered several trenches N. of the CANAL enemy retaliated on front line with pip-squeaks & trench mortars.		
70th Bty.	10.20 am fired at trench mortar at A.21.b.7.8. 10.35 am trench mortar firing from A.15.d.9.0. 2.25 pm tested gun on machine-gun firing at aeroplane 2.40 pm 4 pm & 4.10 pm Registered. A great deal of traffic heard on the main LA BASSEE road last night.		
From Place Time	Observation impossible from 4.45 pm – 8.30 am Light bad all day. Wind W.N.W.		

(Z)   J.H.Lewis 2nd Lieut

DAILY DIARY

Z group R.A.   27-10-15

9th Fired on new machine gun emplacement of Obs. post in 21 d 6.6 putting three shots through it. This and a little registration is all there is to report.

15th Fired on RAILWAY and support trenches, checked lines on trench A22 a 15 to FRANKS keep and trench FRANKS to RYANS keep.

17th Fired on CORON alley at 9am, and on german trenches when the germans fired on our aeroplanes this afternoon.

45th Batt. Nothing to report.

71st Batt registered CHATEAU Alley and retaliated on Mine Point Les Briques etc by request of infantry.

Work reported by 9th Batt was done during night. Germans shelled Vermelles with 10 cm followed by 77 m. 15th Batt Mess windows broken.

Light fair to bad.

Rodd ?
Adj. 41st Bde.

DAILY AMMUNITION RETURN. Roemana 27/10/15

Piece	Projectile	Code	50	70	15	48	71	9	16	17	47	53	Total	Per piece
2.75	Guns													
	Shrapnel	P	15	15	53	–	52	121	51	51	–	1	358	119
	H.E.	PX	18	36	–	–	18	29	–	23	–	1		
18-pr	Guns													
	Shrapnel	A												
	H.E.	AX												
4.5" How.	Howitzers								–	9	–	–	9	
	Special									3	15	–	18	
	Shrapnel	B								12	25	–	37	
	H.E.	BX												
6" How	Howitzers													
	Shrapnel	H												
	H.E.	F												
	A.P.													

1411

2nd Division Artillery Orders

by

Brigadier-General G.H.SANDERS, D.S.O., Comdg.R.A., 2nd Divn.

27th October, 1915.

1069. OFFICER's POSTING.

Lieutenant H.E.BARKWORTH, 56th Battery is appointed Acting Adjutant 44th Brigade; vice Captain H.F.WILLCOCKS to 56th Battery, with effect from 15th October, 1915.

1070. SMOKE HELMETS - USE OF

O.s C.Units are again reminded of the necessity to continually inspect smoke helmmts, and also to assure themselves that the men thoroughly understand how to put them on and use them in their work.

L.G.BUXTON, Capt, R.A.,
Staff Captain, R.A., 2nd Divn.

DAILY DIARY

Z group R.A.   28-10-15

9th Batt. fired on a working party in
22 B 2.5 at 8am. 10.15 am Phizbang
shelled O.P. retaliate on AUCHY house
Fired a M.G. emplacement 3.30pm
21 b 6.3 having previously warned
BERKS.

15th Batt fired on POPES NOSE. 1.30am
17th Batt fired on working party at 9am.
Fired 1rds at working party 2.35pm
at which they dispersed and were
not seen again. Some Retaliation.
47th Batt. Nothing to report.
71st Batt. did some retaliation.

Enemy shelling: BRADDELL point
CAMBRIN support and vicinity were
shelled with 77 m this morning
and this afternoon. This was
probably due to the movement in this
neighborhood and smoke of fires.
Vermelles also was shelled
Retaliation: Germans required
retaliation five times today.
Localities selected were AUCHY

front and support trenches

Some new coil wire has been put up between boyaux 17 & 18 by germans. Infantry report wire is very strong between Boyaux 15 & 17

Reference cloud of smoke seen see special envelope.

Light poor today.

9th Batt move two guns to rear position tonight.

P. Rodd (?)
Adj. 41st Bde

FDA/40

Hqrs. RA II Div.

With Reference to cloud of Smoke :- 17th Batt saw one from A21d79 at 2.30pm no report was heard. It drifted north and quickly dispersed.

O.C 17th Batt considers it may have been a gas cylinder owing to volume but more probably was some form of bomb.

19th Bde report 4 trench mortar bombs fell at 3.45pm which made a large cloud of smoke

Rodd
28-10-15
Adj. 41st Bde

MESSAGES AND SIGNALS.

"A" Form. Army Form C. 2121.

Prefix	Code	m.	Words	Charge	This message is on a/c of:	Recd. at ... m.
Office of Origin and Service Instructions.			Sent		...Service.	Date...
			At ... m.			From...
			To			By...
			By		(Signature of "Franking Officer.")	

TO RA. 2nd Divn.

Sender's Number.	Day of Month.	In reply to Number	AAA
OK/35.	28th		

Daily Report 34th Bde.

50th Bty fired at 5.30 am, 5.40 am, & 6.15 am. at foot of 'embankment REDOUBT' as enemy have been seen working there at dawn recently.

Fired at 9.35 am. & 9.45 am. at working parties, on Railway Embankment A.16.c.5.8. and at A.17.a.3.4. respectively. Parties were dispersed.

70th Bty fired at 10 am, 11.25 am & 3.20 pm on trenches in 'A', in retaliation for pip-squeaks on BARRIER & BRADDELL POINT.

Fired at 10.55 am. on working party at A.21.b.9.8.

Observation impossible from 4.15 pm to 6.30 am.

From: Wind S.W.

Place:

Time: 56th Bty - Did not fire -

A Durand Lt.
Adj. 34th Bde.

The above may be forwarded as now corrected. (Z)

2nd Division Artillery Orders

by

Brigadier-General G.H.SANDERS., D.S.O., Comdg R.A. 2nd Divn.

28th September, 1915.

1015. R.A. ORDERS.

Were not issued yesterday, 27-9-1915.

1016. DISCIPLINE.

The Commander-in-chief regrets to notice a prevalence of the most serious and dangerous offence of "Sleeping on the Post".

It has not been necessary up to the present time to carry out the extreme penalty in relation to this offence but the number of cases which have recently occurred have caused the Commander-in-chief to decide that he will have no alternative but to carry out the extreme penalty in the future.

This order is to be read out on parade three times.

1017. WAR DIARIES.

The War Diaries of brigades should contain all that is necessary to record as regards their individual batteries. Diaries will not be expected from batteries unless they are acting independantly of their Brigade.

L.G. BUXTON. Capt, R.A.,
Staff Captain, R.A. 2nd Divn.

DAILY DIARY
44th Bde RFA
6-6pm. 27th – 28th Oct. 1915.

Operations 56th Bty.

   No firing.

Information Nil

                    W.W. Sankworth
                        Lt AH
                    for Lt.Col. Cmdg 44th Bde

1413

DAILY AMMUNITION RETURN. Expended 28/10/15

Piece	Projectile	Code	50	70	15	48	71	9	16	17	47	55			Total	Per piece
2.75	Guns															
	Shrapnel	P														
	H.E.	PX													2½/35	
18-pr	Guns															
	Shrapnel	A		31	28	39	–	–	53	51	107	63				
	H.E.	AX		34	48	–	–	1	26	15	6	1				
4.5" How.	Howitzers															
	Shrapnel	B														
	H.E.	BX										68				
6" How	Howitzers															
	Shrapnel	H														
	H.E.	F													89	
	A.P.															

1914

2nd Division Artillery Orders

by

Brigadier-General G.H.SANDERS, D.S.O., Comdg.R.A., 2nd Divn.

28th October,1915.

1071. COURTMARTIAL.

A F.G.C.M., composed as under, will assemble at Hd. Qrs, 44th B.A.C.,Rue Gambetta, Bethune, at 10-0 a.m. on Saturday, 30th October,1915, for the trial of 70670, S.S. E. Giddings, 56th Battery, R.F.A., and 32236, Dr.Thistlethwaite, 9th Battery, R.F.A., and such other accused as may be brought before it :-

PRESIDENT.
Major T.N.French.   47th Battery, R.F.A.

MEMBERS.
Captain S.Atkinson.   16th Battery, R.F.A.
Lieut. S.K.Thorburn. 15th Battery, R.F.A.

Accused will be warned and all witnesses duly required to attend.
The 44th Brigade, R.F.A., will detail the Court Orderly and supply the necessary stationery.
Proceedings to be sent to Staff Captain, R.A., 2nd Divn.

1072. LEAVE.

Following is the new allotment of leave :-

Day	Officers	Men	Unit
Friday.	1.	-	D.A.C.
	-	19.	41st Brigade.
Saturday.	2.	-	34th Brigade.
	-	18.	44th "
Sunday.	2.	-	36th Brigade.
	-	18.	D.A.C.
Monday.	1.	-	41st Brigade.
	1.	-	44th "
	-	10.	36th "
	-	4.	7th Mountain Bty
	-	2.	Armoured Cars.
	-	2.	Spare.
Tuesday.	1.	-	41st Brigade.
	1.	-	44th "
	-	9.	41st "
	-	4.	34th "
	-	3.	44th "
	-	2.	D.A.C.
Wednesday.	1.	-	D.A.C.
	-	19.	34th Brigade.
Thursday.	2.	-	34th Brigade.
	-	18.	36th "

L.G.BUXTON, Capt, R.A.,

Staff Captain, R.A., 2nd Divn.

T422

R.A. 2nd Division.
~~R.A. 7th Division.~~

No. 1/R.A./116. 28th Oct.1915.

    Will you please inform me how many 'Wardrop Shields' for 18pr. Q.F. guns are being used in the batteries under your command.

    Also, please state if any more are required.

                                              Major, R.A.
                                  Staff Officer R.A. 1st Corps

"A" Form. Army Form C. 2121.
MESSAGES AND SIGNALS.

TO: RA 1st Corps

Sender's Number: Bm 888
Day of Month: 31
In reply to Number: 1/RA/116
AAA

We have no WARDROP Shields aaa Would like two to keep in case of need aaa

From: RA 2 Div
Time: 5.55 pm

"A" Form.
MESSAGES AND SIGNALS.
Army Form C. 2121.

TO	R.A. 2nd Div.

Sender's Number.	Day of Month.	In reply to Number	AAA
O.K. 41	29th.		

Observation impossible from 4.20 pm – 7.45 am. Wind SOUTH.

Enemy's artillery have been much more active to-day. A great deal of pip-squeaking on main road from HARLEY ST to BRIGADE HDQRS.

A shell at S.E. corner of "A" Brickstack this morning caused a large cloud of white vapour to rise from the German trenches.

What appears to be 2 very tall observation ladders have been seen in the trees at approx^t A.17.c.0.4. A man was seen descending one. Owing to bad light they were only occasionally visible, & a close watch is being kept to locate them accurately.

A. Durand /f.
39th Bde.

MESSAGES AND SIGNALS.

"A" Form.
Army Form C. 2121.

TO R.A. 2nd Division

Sender's Number: OK/41
Day of Month: 29th
AAA

<u>Daily Report 34th Bde</u>

50th Bty — At 5am and 5.30am fired at foot of EMBANKMENT REDOUBT as enemy have been seen working there lately at dawn. During morning and at 3.20 pm enemy's Artillery intermittently shelled the HOLLOW and our front line trenches. 56th Bty retaliated on trenches

70th Bty — At 5 pm & 9pm last night fired on AUCHY & HAISNES in retaliation to shelling of CAMBRIN & HARLEY ST. At 9.30 a.m & 11.30 a.m fired on AUCHY and trenches respectively in retaliation to pip-squeaks. from 12-12.30 registered trenches N. of Canal. At 1.55 pm fired on trenches as enemy were shooting at aeroplane. At 11.30 pm & 10.57am retaliated to MINENWERFER in BRICKFIELDS

From
Place 56 R By
Time

At 2.15 pm continued registration N. of CANAL

DAILY DIARY

Z group R.A.   29-10-15

9th Batt. fired a few rounds in retaliation and registered 2 guns from rear position.

15th Batt. fired on Minenwerfer 10.50am

17th Batt fired in retaliation.

47th How Batt registered TORTOISE

71st Batt fired on MINE point by request; and House A23 c 9.3.

Enemy very active shelling all day all over Z group front and down La Bassée road. Direct hits were scored on Maison Rouge Four hundred Braddell Castle etc. Also shelled + roads E Vermelles. At same time it should be noted ① 1st Berks ran a hand wheeled cart with hurdles right up to Barrier ② a working party of 1/62 Batt shewed itself very conspicuously near Curragh Grange ③ a new trench is being dug near "400". This may account for

This may account in part for this distressing shelling.

Enemy have strengthened wire of trenches in A 2 B B and D considerably.

Rodd A.
Adj 41st Bd.

DAILY AMMUNITION RETURN.

29.X.15

Piece	Projectile	Code	BATTERIES									Total	Per piece
			50	70	15	48	71	9	16	17	47	56		
2.75	Guns													
	Shrapnel	P												
	H.E.	PX												
18-pr	Guns													
	Shrapnel	A	11	32	16	-	17	58	81	36			251	
	H.E.	AX	1	40	-	-	22	43	-	10			116	
4.5" How.	Howitzers													
	Shrapnel	B										13	13	
	H.E.	BX												
6" How	Howitzers													
	Shrapnel	H												
	H.E.	F												
	A.P.													

2nd Division Artillery Orders

by

Brigadier-General G.H.SANDERS, D.S.O., Comdg R.A., 2nd Div.

29th October, 1915.

1073. COURTMARTIAL.

No.66141. Corporal A.Hallam, 70th Battery, R.F.A., will be brought before the F.G.C.M., ordered to assemble in R.A.Order No.1071, dated 28-10-1915.

L.G.BUXTON, Capt, R.A.
Staff Captain, R.A., 2nd Divn.

DAILY DIARY.

2 group R.A.   30-10-15

9th Batt. fired on OP in AUCHY 23 a 2.5 which made firing on CAMBRIN stop at once 7.45 am. Registration from rear position was continued. Germans were fired on at intervals when seen B.19 a 0.5

10th Batt. fired on Mad Point 3.35 pm.

17th Batt. besides some retaliation fired on a German working party in PEKIN trench; also on another digging a trench N. of Diamond Door cottage.

47th How. Batt. fired on Ryans heap to stop Minenwerfers and also in retaliation to some shell on our trenches.

B Batt fired on trench A 21 d 3.4, and retaliated on houses in AUCHY and on 1st & second line trenches.

ENEMY shelling. Germans shelled CAMBRIN and trenches with 77 mm also Support trench A 27 d with 105 mm.

WORK. Enemy have slightly altered and done work on parapet in 21 d 7.8. Here a periscope has been seen recently. This place, probably an O.B. was demolished by 9th Batt

A german seen wearing a "Brodrick" cap with a red Triangle in front is reported by O C 9th Batt.

Rodd th
Adj. 41st Bn.

"A" Form. Army Form C.2121.
MESSAGES AND SIGNALS.   No. of Message

Prefix	Code	m.	Words	Charge	This message is on a/c of:	Recd. at	m.
Office of Origin and Service Instructions.			Sent			Date	
			At	m.	Service.	From	
			To			By	
			By		(Signature of "Franking Officer.")		

TO: R.A. 2nd Division

| Sender's Number. | Day of Month. | In reply to Number | AAA |
| OK/47 | 30th | | |

Daily Report 34th Bde.—

50th Bty. Enemy's artillery fired during most of the day. 50th Bty retaliated on EMBANKMENT REDOUBT and N.E. BRICKSTACK

70th Bty. At 10.30 am fired on Germans seen pulling down timber from Ruins at A22 8.48. At 2.55 pm and 4.33 pm fired on 1st & 2nd line trenches in retaliation. At 3.55 pm 3 Foreign Attachés, 2 Japanese & 1 Russian visited the Battery & each fired a round. No movement seen at Obs. Ladders upwards of today

From
Place
Time

"A" Form.   Army Form C. 2121.

MESSAGES AND SIGNALS.

No. of Message _____

Prefix ____ Code ____ m.	Words	Charge	This message is on a/c of:	Recd. at ____ m.
Office of Origin and Service Instructions.				Date ____
	Sent		_____ Service.	From ____
	At ____ m.			
	To ____			By ____
	By ____		(Signature of "Franking Officer.")	

TO { R.A. 2nd Division

Sender's Number.	Day of Month.	In reply to Number	AAA
6R/47			

5?? Bty Retaliated to MINENWERFER at 'D' BRICK STACK at 11.30pm. From 9.56 – 10.15am fired shrapnel at houses at A22 c.99. No movement has been observed.

50th & 56th Btys completed registration of trenches N. of CANAL
Observation impossible between 4.20pm and 7.15 am.
Wind Slight – S.W.

a/ Sloan Lieut
a/ Adj 34th Bde

From			
Place			
Time			

The above may be forwarded as now corrected.   (Z)

Censor.   Signature of Addressor or person authorised to telegraph in his name.

* This line should be erased if not required.

1419

DAILY AMMUNITION RETURN.

30.X.15

Piece	Projectile	Code	\multicolumn{10}{c	}{BATTERIES}	Total	Per Piece
			30	70	15	48	71	9	16	17	47	56		
18-pr	Guns	48												
	Shrapnel	A	40	19	-	-	15	106	41	65			286	
	H. E.	Ax	1	20	-	-	3	92	-	-			116	
4.5" (Howzr)	Howitzers	12												
	Shrapnel	B									10		10	
	H. E.	Bx								20	39		59	

2nd Division Artillery Orders

by

Brigadier-General G.H.SANDERS, D.S.O., Comdg R.A., 2nd Divn.

30th October, 1915.

1074. SIGNALLING CLASS.

2nd Division Signals can only take five men per Brigade for the Signalling Class. These men should report to O.C. 2nd Divn. Signals at 10-0 a.m. on Monday, November 1st, at the Ecole Des Garcons, Bethune. They will be rationed by 2nd Divn. Signals from and including that date, until their instruction is completed. They will not be paid by 2nd Divn. Signals.

1075. CLIPPERS, HORSE

The attention of all concerned is drawn to General Routine Order No. 1234, dated 29th October, 1915.

1076. REMOUNTS.

Return showing number of remounts required to complete establishment, should be rendered to this office by 9 a.m. on the 12th and 26th day of each month.

1077. DIVINE SERVICE.

All units R.F.A., in or near BETHUNE will attend divine service in New Chapel, opposite civil prison, at 9-30 a.m. to-morrow.

1078. AMMUNITION.

O's C. Units will ensure that all echelons are full to-morrow.

L.G.BUXTON, Capt, R.A.,
Staff Captain, R.A., 2nd Divn.

"A" Form. Army Form C. 2121.

MESSAGES AND SIGNALS.

Prefix ... Code ... m.	Words	Charge	This message is on a/c of:	Recd. at ... m.
Office of Origin and Service Instructions.	Sent			Date
	At ... m.		Service.	From
	To			By
	By		(Signature of "Franking Officer.")	

TO { R.A. 2nd Div.

| Sender's Number. | Day of Month. | In reply to Number | AAA |
| OR/51 | 31st | | |

	Daily Report 34th Bde.		
50th Bty	11 am Registered point on north bank of CANAL possible Snipers post.		
	2.45 pm. Enemy fired on our communication trenches south of BERKSHIRE LANE with field & heavy howitzers. Retaliated on N E BRICKSTACK		
70th Bty	Fired 2.35 pm on 1st & 2nd line trenches in retaliation for 4.2 falling just N. of MOUNTAIN HOUSE orchard close to our communication trenches		
56th Bty	Did not fire		

All very quiet on our front
The Enemy has strengthened trench on lip of embankment redoubt
Observation impossible 4.30 pm – 8 am
Light very bad all day wind S.E.

From
Place
Time

The above may be forwarded as now corrected. (Z)

J.W. Lewis 2nd Lieut.

Censor. Signature of Addresser or person authorised to telegraph in his name.

* This line should be erased if not required.

DAILY DIARY

Z group RA.   31-10-15

9th Batt fired on Germans in any B.19.a.0.5
and on working party A.22.a.2.3

15th Batt on Minenwerfer near
MINE point this morning.

17th Batt fired on German working
party A.29.a.7.6.

47th How. Batt. fired on RYANS KEEP
and A.21.d.7.1 by request of infantry
last night and this morning.

1st Batt fired on German front
& support trenches in retaliation
to minenwerfers and bombs
also shelled area A.21.d.7.1. & 7.3.

Very quiet day all day

Some new sandbags seen A.22.a.2.3
and wire in triangle in A.28 (centre)
has been further strengthened.

Rodd K.
Adj. 41st Bde

DAILY AMMUNITION RETURN.

31 Oct 15

Piece	Projectile	Code	BATTERIES											Total	Per Piece
			30	70	15	48	71	9	16	17	47	56			
18-pr	Guns	48													
	Shrapnel	A	49	7	8	-	16	31	55	84				250	
	H. E.	Ax	-	13	14	-	30	10	-	55				122	
4.5" (Howzr)	Howitzers	12													
	Shrapnel	B									5			5	
	H. E.	Bx									24			24	

1423

www.ingramcontent.com/pod-product-compliance
Lightning Source LLC
Chambersburg PA
CBHW080843010526
44114CB00017B/2359